SUNKEN GARDENS

A Step-by-Step Guide to Planting Freshwater Aquariums

Karen A. Randall

TIMBER PRESS

Portland, Oregon

Published in 2016 by Timber Press, Inc.

The Haseltine Building
133 S.W. Second Avenue, Suite 450
Portland, Oregon 97204-3527
timberpress.com

Printed in China

Text design by Will Brown
Cover design by Kristi Pfeffer
Illustrations by Kate Francis

Library of Congress Cataloging-in-Publication Data

Names: Randall, Karen A., author.
Title: Sunken gardens: a step-by-step guide to planting freshwater aquariums
    / Karen A. Randall.
Other titles: Step by step guide to planting freshwater aquariums
Description: Portland, Oregon: Timber Press, 2016. | Includes
    bibliographical references and index.
Identifiers: LCCN 2016021286 | ISBN 9781604695922 (pbk.)
Subjects: LCSH: Aquarium plants. | Aquarium animals. | Aquariums. | Water
    gardens.
Classification: LCC SF457.7 (print) | DDC 639.8—dc23
LC record available at https://lccn.loc.gov/2016021286

A catalog record for this book is also available from the British Library.

CONTENTS

PREFACE

Aquatic gardening, or the keeping of planted aquariums as opposed to "fish tanks," is a pastime that has grown by leaps and bounds in the 21st century. Previously, those of us who were interested in planted aquariums had to be pretty inventive about finding and making the equipment and supplies needed to be successful with our aquatic gardens.

Today, many sources of good quality, commercially made equipment, substrates, and fertilizers exist. There are internet communities where planted aquariums are discussed and debated, and articles in general aquarium magazines that address the interests of planted aquarium enthusiasts. With so much information available—some great, some not so great—it can be difficult for the novice to sort through. Even among the good information, a number of different though valid approaches exist that can be confusing for the beginner. Each of these methods may work well, but if a beginner starts mixing techniques, he or she can become hopelessly confused and end up with an empty tank for sale at the end of the driveway.

Aquatic gardening is a chance to garden year-round in your home.

Outside the aquarium world, the term *aquatic gardening* is not well known. Common questions when someone sees their first really beautiful planted tank are, "Are those plants real?" or "Is that a saltwater tank?" People are often surprised that a freshwater aquarium can be so beautiful. Among terrestrial gardeners, aquatic gardening brings to mind the garden pond: a lovely garden but a different type of gardening altogether.

My hope in this book is to introduce readers to the fascinating world of the planted aquarium. For those who come from a terrestrial gardening background, the planted aquarium is a perfect extension of your hobby: a way to keep your thumb green even through long cold winters. For those of you who are fish aquarists and want to expand into the world of planted tanks, you will find them to be not only a very interesting addition to your aquariums, but they provide a much better environment for your fish. And for those who are brand new to it all, I hope this book opens a door into a world of wonder for you.

Happy (and wet) gardening!

1

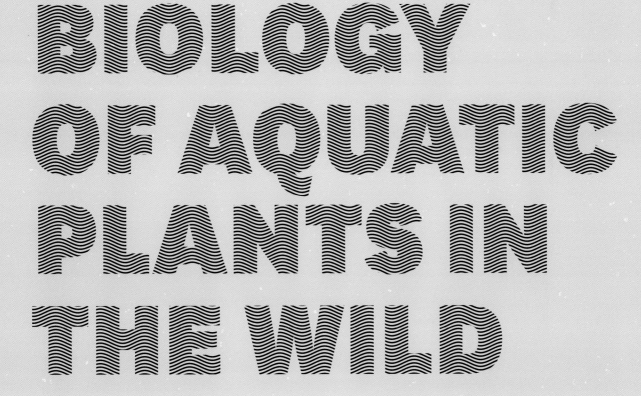

BIOLOGY OF AQUATIC PLANTS IN THE WILD

WHILE WE OFTEN refer to the plants that we use in aquariums as "aquatic plants," they actually range from fully aquatic species that live entirely underwater to amphibious species that spend part of the time under water (submersed) and part of the time above water (emersed). Sometimes this is seasonal, based on the depth of the water at various times of year. Other times, it simply depends on where the plant happens to be growing.

Some plants can take full advantage of either damp ground or submersed conditions. Others grow with their roots either in the substrate or in the water column and have floating leaves. Still others grow completely floating on the surface. Plants with all of these growth patterns are represented among the plants that do well in the aquarium.

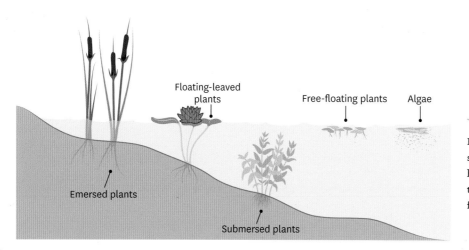

Floating-leaved plants

Free-floating plants

Algae

Emersed plants

Submersed plants

Plants in the littoral zone (the shallow area in a river or lake) have a variety of growth patterns and are suitable choices for an aquarium.

WHY PLANTS GROW WHERE THEY DO

Cryptocoryne cordata is an example of a plant that has adapted to grow where many other plants cannot. This particular variety, from southern Thailand, can take advantage of areas that are not only shady, but also have relatively deep hard water.

One thing that is absolutely essential to plant growth is adequate light. Some aquatic plant species have adapted to grow in shady settings. Among them are many ferns and mosses as well as *Anubias* species and many *Cryptocoryne* species. These plants have been the long-term mainstays of the aquarium world because they grow well even under fairly dim aquarium lighting.

Other species grow wild in open areas with shallow, clear water. These plants, in general, are much more demanding in the aquarium, needing much higher light levels to thrive. Many of the most beautiful and brightly colored aquarium plants are in this category and are well worth the extra effort required to maintain them.

These tiny threadlike leaves are the first produced by *Cryptocoryne crispatula* along the Mekong River in Thailand as the water recedes at the end of the rainy season. The plant cannot photosynthesize in the deep, turbid waters of the river during high water periods.

Here is the same form of *Cryptocoryne crispatula* growing in the same area, but now fully emersed.

What you will not find in the wild are plants growing for long periods in very deep or muddy water. Such water does not allow enough light to pass through for plants to grow.

Some plants do grow in areas where the water is deep and turbid for parts of the year, but these plants typically lose their leaves when water conditions rob them of light, and then regrow their leaves and start to flower when water levels drop, the current slows, and the water becomes clearer. While adaptive in the wild, this behavior is obviously undesirable in an aquarium plant.

Soon, *Cryptocoryne crispatula* sends up its distinctive flower spikes. While the Mekong form of the species shown here is not a suitable aquarium plant because of this growth habit, there are other varieties of *C. crispatula* that make exemplary aquarium plants.

Even in areas where the water is far harder than any tap water, you can find successful plant species. This is a beautiful spot called El Trampolín in Tamasopo, San Luis Potosí, Mexico.

This lovely green form of *Ludwigia palustris* is just one of a number of beautiful plants found at El Trampolín.

There are only a few places in the world where you can find entire rivers of clear, running water filled with healthy plants. This is the Thodupuzha River, a beautiful and very soft water river in India, home to a wide variety of plants used in aquariums.

A tributary to the Kwai River in western Thailand is a moderately hard water river, and home to the wildly popular *Pogostemon helferi*, commonly called "downoi," the pink flowers visible on the rocks. While it is low water at this point in the year, at high water, these rocks and even most of this small tree are completely submerged in fast flowing, turbid water in the rainy season.

Few aquarium plants are found along the Amazon River and its larger tributaries due to huge fluctuations in water depth and color, which ranges from the color of tea to "white water" areas the color of café au lait in most areas. With the exception of a few clear-water rivers, little light is available for plant growth except at the surface of the water, where plants like these enormous *Victoria amazonica* lilies are found.

WHAT PEOPLE CAN DO TO SUPPORT NATURAL SPACES

Native plants and animals often suffer from habitat degradation and competition for resources due to the introduction of nonnative species. Unfortunately, especially in the warmer parts of the United States as well as other parts of the world, invasive nonnative aquatic plants are playing havoc with waterways, crowding out native plant species, destroying areas where animals reproduce, and in some cases, causing dangerous conditions for water fowl which become trapped in floating plants. Our responsibility to our natural spaces is to prevent the spread of invasive species.

Invasive species aren't a problem only in the United States. *Myriophyllum aquaticum*, a South American native, is commonly found in tropical areas in Asia where it becomes invasive. In the United States, two of most problematic invasive aquatic plants are Eurasian watermilfoil, *Myriophyllum spicatum*, which can now be found over most of the country, and *Hydrilla verticillata*. This second plant, once thought to be mostly a warm water invader, has proven much more cold tolerant than expected, and can now be found as far north as Connecticut and the Finger Lakes in New York.

While aquarists aren't the only or even the main cause of invasive nonnatives in waterways, it is vitally important that they do not contribute to the problem. Make sure that you know your local and federal laws. Do not use plants that are considered invasive weeds in your area (This can vary widely, depending on the climate.) But even with plants that are legal, do not take chances on them escaping. It can take just a small amount of some plants to allow them to become established in the wild. Do not dump aquarium contents anywhere near bodies of water or wetlands. And do your part to educate others about the need to protect our waterways.

On the flip side of the coin, the United States is home to a number of wonderful aquarium-worthy species. It is great fun to go out and study these plants in the wild, observing their native habitat, photographing them, and even collecting them for our tanks. But again, it is very important to observe all local laws. Check with your local fish and wildlife department for guidance before doing any collecting. Make sure you know of any threatened or endangered species, and leave these strictly alone. Most threatened and endangered plants are vulnerable because of habitat degradation, so do your part to avoid damaging the environment in any way.

Myriophyllum aquaticum, a native to South America, has become established in many of the warmer areas of the world. Here it clogs a stream in Thailand. While it is a pretty aquarium plant (and also used in garden ponds), it is very invasive, and care must be taken that it doesn't escape into the wild.

Water hyacinth, *Eichhornia crassipes*, is another South American plant that has become a huge problem as an invasive around the world. Although it is not used in aquariums, it is often used as a floating plant in ornamental ponds.

Hydrilla verticillata is an invasive nonnative in the southeastern United States, where it costs huge amounts of money to control each year. In the photo, growing where it should in a stream in southern Thailand, the same species doesn't take over, is lovely to look at, and makes a wonderful cover for small, spawning fish.

Many habitats in the United States are worth exploring for worthy aquarium subjects. Several interesting species were found under this overpass above a river.

Members of the Greater Washington Aquatic Plant Association rediscovered the "real" *Sagittaria subulata*. It turned out that the plant known by this name in the hobby for many years was the wrong plant. This one is a much nicer aquarium plant and grows into a lovely grassy ground cover under good conditions. It is now available, propagated and traded between aquatic gardeners.

Most aquarium plants sold today come from commercial nurseries in the United States, Europe, and Southeast Asia. Here Claus Christensen, former director of Tropica Aquarium Plants in Denmark, and Brad McLean, owner of Florida Aquatic Nurseries, share ideas at Brad's nursery in 2010.

Do not collect in state or federal parks, where this activity is almost universally prohibited. When on private land, make sure you have the land owner's permission. That is often easy to obtain by simply asking, but do people that courtesy.

And remember that if a plant is going to do well in an aquarium, you do not need a lot of it to start with. Many plants that are going to grow in your aquarium will typically do so quickly, and you will soon be weeding them out of your tank to share with friends. Other species may require a more experienced aquarist to get them established. You will become more successful with finicky plants over time if working with native plants interests you.

Please avoid purchasing wild-collected plants, as they are a drain on the environment. Most plants that are worthy of aquarium use become available commercially.

2

BASIC AQUARIUM WATER CHEMISTRY

YOU CAN SKIP this chapter for now if it makes your eyes cross, but you'll appreciate it later. It is the most (and I hope the only) boring chapter in this book, but it's very important. So I hope that even if you skip ahead for now in favor of the fun stuff, you'll come back to it later. Hopefully you will do this *before* you get in trouble.

TAP WATER

The clear stuff that comes out of your faucet has a lot of different, invisible things in it—some good and some not so good. Other substances in tap water are neither absolutely good nor bad but need to be carefully considered because of their effect on aquarium plants and animals.

It is much easier to learn how to grow a beautiful planted tank if you first understand what is in your tap water and how to deal with it.

Don't be discouraged if your tap water falls outside the ideal range for planted tanks. This lovely tank by Tony Gomez, which is planted mostly with *Cryptocoryne* sp., is in an area of the country with extremely hard water. The aquarist has chosen to use species that will do well in the water he has rather than fight to change the water chemistry. The result is a tank that's not only pretty, but easy to maintain.

The first thing to do if you want to avoid problems with your planted tank is to get a printout of your tap water chemistry from your local water department. My town sends these out automatically, twice a year, but if yours doesn't, it is still required, by federal law, to provide you with a copy upon request.

If you have a private well, you will need to hire someone to do a chemical analysis of your water, but you have to do that periodically to ensure the safety of your drinking water anyway. This basic information helps you determine what, if anything, you need to add to your water to make it suitable for a planted tank, and may affect how much fertilizer you use.

In general, it is best to learn to garden with the water you have rather than try to make drastic changes. Long experience has taught me that people who work too hard to change their basic, out-of-the-tap water chemistry often cause themselves greater headaches than if they left it alone. They also rarely continue with this level of work in the long term. Fortunately, in most, if not all, areas of the country you can grow beautiful plants in water from the tap as long as you chose the right species and don't get hung up on the plants that don't like local water conditions.

Chlorine/Chloramine

Unless you have a private well, the chances are that your local municipality adds chlorine or chloramine to the tap water to make it safe for humans to drink. Unfortunately, both of these substances are toxic to fish and invertebrates.

Chloramine is more often used today than chlorine because it is more stable. A few water departments still use chlorine, but they can change at any time, and they do not have to notify you when the change is made. Since chloramine is harder to deal with, and the treatment for chloramine will also effectively treat chlorine, we will discuss the treatment of chloramine.

Commercial chloramine neutralizers are widely available, usually in the form of bottled liquid. Look for a product that specifically states that it will neutralize chloramine, not just chlorine. I strongly suggest that you treat all water going into your aquarium unless you are using water from a private well and are certain that no chlorine or chloramine is used.

If the levels of chlorine or chloramine in your tap water are low, the treatment won't cause any harm. If they are high (and this can happen unexpectedly, especially in the summer), the treatment will save the lives of your fish. In most cases, you can add the chloramine neutralizer directly to the aquarium just before you add the tap water. Some "water treatment" products make claims about doing all sorts of other beneficial things to your tap water. These are not necessary for a healthy tank, and are more marketing hype than anything else. Some can actually be detrimental.

General Hardness

In some areas of the country, the water is extremely hard, meaning that there are a lot of minerals dissolved in it, most often calcium and magnesium. Hardness can be measured as German degrees of hardness (dGH), parts per million (ppm), or milligrams per liter (mg/L). Parts per million and milligrams per liter are analogous and are often used interchangeably in aquarists' discussions. Most test kits typically measure calcium and magnesium, usually the largest mineral components to hard water.

Rio Sabinas in Hidalgo, Mexico, is a hard water river which is home to a good variety of old-time favorites in the aquarium hobby. Here, in the foreground, you can see a field of *Shinnersia rivularis*, Mexican oakleaf, flowering along the shallow, sandy shoreline.

Another measure is total dissolved solids (TDS), which quantifies all (or most of) the minerals dissolved in the water, no matter what they are. Electrical conductivity measures the water's ability to transmit and electrical current. Most aquarists don't bother much with conductivity or even total dissolved solids, preferring to measure hardness by degrees, parts per million, or milligrams per liter.

From a homeowner's perspective, very hard water leaves a residue on silverware, glassware, and appliances; deposits in pipes and faucets; and can make it hard for soap to do its job in the laundry. Many people in areas with very hard water install whole house water softeners. These devices typically replace calcium carbonate in the tap water with sodium chloride, although a few units use potassium chloride instead.

The problem with replacing one molecule with a different one is that although the amount of calcium and magnesium may go down, the amount of sodium goes up by the same amount. Many plants can't tolerate much sodium in the water, and fish that do better in soft water will have no easier time in sodium-filled water than they would in water with high levels of calcium. What is important to fish is the total dissolved solids, which doesn't change when you exchange one molecule for another.

If you live in a hard water area and have a whole-house water softener system, make sure you install a bypass for the softener, and use unsoftened tap water for your aquarium. Your plants will thank you, and most fish will too.

Plants need a certain amount of calcium and magnesium for proper growth. A good range for general hardness is between 50 and 150 mg/L. If your hardness is lower than 50 mg/L, you can increase it by adding calcium carbonate to your aquarium.

One of the easiest ways to increase water hardness is to add a small filter bag of aragonite or crushed coral (substrates marketed for marine aquariums) to your filter. The substrate will slowly dissolve, adding a steady source of both hardness and carbonate hardness (discussed later) to your water. You can also add these substances to your substrate, but hardness is harder to control that way. If the substances are added to the filter, you can always remove them or reduce the amount if you find that the water is getting too hard. This method is best used in aquariums not receiving carbon dioxide (CO_2) enrichment.

The acidification of the water by CO_2 and the rapid water flow through the filter may cause the aragonite to dissolve too quickly, increasing the hardness and the buffering capacity (alkalinity) of the water more than you want. If supplemental CO_2 is used, then it works well to hang a fine mesh bag of aragonite in an area of the aquarium with less water flow and where it can be easily removed. There are also commercial products available that can be added with each water change to increase the carbonate hardness, general hardness, or both.

While hard water will, to some extent, limit the kinds of plants you can grow in your tank, aquarists in Europe successfully grow beautiful planted tanks in water with hardness exceeding 300 mg/L. Even in areas with very hard water, there are plants that can be grown successfully. It is just a matter of choosing the right ones. I still strongly advise that you learn to use the water you have before trying to change your tap water chemistry significantly, at least in the beginning.

If, after you learn what you can grow in your tap water, you decide that you really need to grow species that must have softer water, there are a few options. If you have a small tank, the easiest way to soften the water is to purchase bottled water at the grocery store. Figure out how much tap water you need to mix with the bottled water to achieve the hardness level you desire.

~~~~~~~~~

A view of some of the many species represented in a small stretch of Rio Sabinas.

Some people collect rain water to mix with their tap water, but you need to have a good method of preventing unwanted chemicals from getting into this water, or it can cause more problems than it solves. Collected rain water also often attracts unwanted mosquitos to the yard.

If you need to prepare water for large or multiple tanks, you may want to invest in RO (reverse osmosis) or DI (de-ionization) systems. These expensive filtration systems are only for someone who is very serious about aquatic gardening and has a severe hard water problem. For most of us, learning to garden successfully with the tap water available is a much better option.

Carbonate Hardness

Carbonate hardness is a measure of the amount of carbonates and bicarbonates in the water. These substances buffer the water and allow you to add carbon dioxide (CO_2) to your tank without causing the pH to fall too low. Like general hardness, carbonate hardness can be measured either as parts per million (ppm), milligrams per liter (mg/L), or degrees of carbonate hardness (dKH, or KH, which is an old German measurement).

It is unusual to have a water source that has adequate general hardness and is too low in carbonate hardness, but it does occasionally happen. If your water has less carbonate hardness than you need after adjusting the general hardness, you can increase the carbonate hardness alone by using plain baking soda (sodium bicarbonate). A little less than ¼ teaspoon of baking soda will raise the KH of 10 gallons of water by approximately 1 degree (17.8 mg/L). Do this slowly, in a bucket outside the aquarium until you have a good handle on exactly how much you need.

Be very, very careful about using commercial aquarium buffers in the planted aquarium. Many of these products are based on phosphate compounds and can cause algae problems. At the very least, they will render the KH/pH/CO_2 chart (see side bar page 000) inaccurate to the point of uselessness. In my opinion, phosphate-based buffers are not a good idea in any aquarium and I urge you stick to products containing calcium carbonate or sodium bicarbonate for adjustments.

Test Kits

There are a few test kits that every aquarist should have on hand. You don't need to have a chemistry degree to handle this, so don't worry. You may read arguments online about which test kits are better/more accurate/more expensive. While it is true that scientific-grade reagents and testing protocols will give you the most accurate information in absolute numbers, for our purposes, close is good enough. We will be looking for trends rather than absolute numbers.

One important thing to remember about test kits is that reagents don't age well. So buy from a manufacturer that includes an expiration date on the package, and replace your reagents before that date. It is likely that once you get the hang of running your tank, reagents will go bad before you use them up. That's okay. It's a sign that you have learned to "read your plants," so have less need to rely on test kits.

The bare minimum in terms of test kits for your aquarium should include the following:

Ammonia and nitrite tests. You will probably want to use these two kits in the beginning, especially if you are going to include fish or other animals in your aquarium. Both ammonia and nitrite (not to be confused with nitrate) are very toxic to animals in the aquarium, and are often produced during the first stages of a new tank "cycling."

Nitrate. This kit is useful for two reasons. Once the tank has cycled, if you have fish in it, a rising nitrate level can signify that you are overfeeding or overstocking your tank, or that you are not changing the water often enough. It doesn't hurt to have moderately high levels of nitrate, but high nitrate is a good marker of any waste products accumulating in your water. Nitrate is also an important nutrient for plants. If you can't measure any nitrate in the tank, your plants will suffer.

pH. This measures the acidity or alkalinity (not to be confused with carbonate hardness, which is often incorrectly called alkalinity) of your water.

General hardness. This kit measures the amount of calcium and magnesium in in your water.

Carbonate hardness. This kit measures the carbonate/bicarbonate in your water.

Phosphate. Phosphate is not normally monitored in fish tanks, because it is not particularly damaging to fish. However, because it is a very important plant nutrient, it is measured to make sure there is enough present. Too much phosphate, if not balanced with other nutrients, can cause algae problems.

Nitrate and Phosphate

Another aspect of tap water to keep in mind is whether nitrate or phosphate is present. In agricultural areas, it is not uncommon to have both, due to agricultural run-off. In cities, nitrate is less common, but phosphate compounds are often added to coat old lead water pipes to keep the lead from leaching into the drinking water. You will, in most cases, need to feed your planted tanks with both nitrate and phosphate, but it is important to know what you are adding with water changes, so that you can take this into consideration when dosing nutrients.

pH

pH is a measurement of the acidity or alkalinity of water. These are not accurate terms, but they are the ones you will find most often in hobby literature. There is much more chemistry involved in pH than you need to know for aquarium use, and if you are interested, there are many sites on the internet that can explain it in more detail.

For the aquarium, what you need to know is that a neutral pH is 7.0. Anything below that becomes more acidic, while anything above that is more basic, or alkaline. A pH of 6.0 is 10 times more acidic than 7.0, and a pH of 8.0 is 10 times more alkaline.

Very few bodies of freshwater fall outside the range between 6.0 and 8.0. For planted tanks, we usually work in a range of about 6.4 to 7.4. (Note that ammonia becomes increasingly more toxic above 7.0 so if your aquarium is running at a higher pH, you need to watch the ammonia levels even more closely in the beginning.)

CARBON DIOXIDE

Without the plants that cover our earth, both terrestrial and aquatic, the atmosphere would not contain enough oxygen for us to breathe. We can use the oxygen-producing capabilities of plants to create a healthier environment for our fish in a tank.

Photosynthesis is at the very heart of the food chain. Plants (and certain bacteria) have the unique ability to directly harness the sun's energy. This energy is used to convert water, carbon dioxide (CO_2), and minerals in the environment into organic material in the form of plant growth. A by-product of this process is gaseous oxygen.

The process of photosynthesis is quite complex and beyond the scope of this book. Those who are interested (and it is a very interesting process) can consult the internet or any good encyclopedia. For our purposes, the important part to understand is that for optimal growth (and optimal oxygen production), plants must have a light source that is of adequate intensity, spectrum, and duration (see chapter 3). They must have access to a continuous supply of CO_2 during the hours that the tank is lit, and they must have a reliable supply of all the other nutrients they need.

As with all forms of life, carbon is the substance that the plants need in the largest quantities. In fact, carbon accounts for about 43 percent of the dry weight of all plants. The need for carbon is something we rarely think about with terrestrial plants, as they have access to all the CO_2 they need from the atmosphere.

For aquatic plants, things get a bit harder. Air has a much higher concentration of CO_2 than does water. In large bodies of water, and especially those that are moving, although the amount of dissolved CO_2 is quite low, plants have constant access. The supply is endless.

In some places, even in the wild, the level of dissolved CO_2 in the water is not sufficient for growth so some specialized plants have evolved other strategies for meeting this essential need. The most common way for aquatic and amphibious plants to meet their carbon needs in CO_2—restricted settings is to grow floating or emergent leaves. This bypasses the problem of CO_2 in the water entirely. For our purposes, though, emersed growth and floating leaves can cause problems by blocking much-needed light from the plants below them.

Some plants have the ability to meet their carbon needs by splitting carbon directly from carbonates in the water. These tend to be plants adapted to very hard water environments. While this is a useful adaptation in the wild, it is undesirable in the aquarium. When plants draw on the calcium carbonate in the water to meet their carbon needs (sometimes called biogenic decalcification), the water has

Even in this hard water, high pH river, a constant low-level supply of CO_2 flowing past the plants is sufficient to not only support good growth, but also allow this *Riccia fluitans* to "pearl" (give off excess oxygen). ◄

less and less buffering capacity, leading to serious pH fluctuations. Eventually, the plants can totally exhaust this carbon source as well. A few plants can extract CO_2 from the substrate via specialized roots, but these plants are not commonly used in the aquarium.

Since we know how important CO_2 is for plant growth, we need to decide how we will provide adequate levels to support that growth. There are several natural sources of CO_2 within the aquarium. While plants use CO_2 during photosynthesis, they also return some of it to the water via respiration. During the day, they use much more CO_2 than they produce. At night, there is some build-up of CO_2 when the plants are no longer photosynthesizing. The fish also add to the CO_2 levels in the water with their respiration. The bacterial decay of dead plant material, driftwood decorations in the tank, and the biofilter produces CO_2.

In a properly stocked, moderately lit tank without aeration during the day, it is possible to have reasonably good growth without supplemental CO_2 if you choose the right plants. At higher light levels, CO_2 supplementation becomes increasingly necessary. Measure the pH in the morning before the lights come on, and again in the late afternoon. If the pH is significantly increased, it is a signal that the plants are using up all available CO_2 in the tank. If the alkalinity (or carbonate hardness) of the tank drops over time, carbon deprivation is almost a certainty.

One way that plants solve the problem of accessing enough CO_2 is by extracting it from the atmosphere. That is what this emergent *Pontederia* (pickerel weed) and the floating leaves of the surrounding *Potomogeton* (pond weed) have done in a small pond in Massachusetts. Here, the lack of water flow exhausts the dissolved CO_2 in the water column much faster than in a flowing stream. ►

If you have any question whether a tank can benefit from the addition of CO_2, compare this photo with the next one. The photos show the same tank a couple of months apart. The only difference between the two photos is the addition of a yeast reactor between the times the photos were taken. This provided just a small amount of CO_2, and the growth difference is remarkable.

The same tank after the addition of supplemental CO_2 shows significant plant growth.

The safe and effective starting range for CO_2 in the aquarium for good plant growth is 20 to 30 mg/L. Some people are able to push this higher if it is increased slowly and carefully. CO_2 levels can also be kept much higher in a tank that does not contain any fish.

Novice aquatic gardeners are often concerned that adding CO_2 to their tanks will limit the amount of oxygen available for their fish. At the levels we target in the aquarium, oxygen and CO_2 coexist. Adding small amounts of CO_2 does not displace oxygen. In fact, proper use of supplemental CO_2 with appropriate lighting and fertilization should actually increase the level of dissolved oxygen in the water. Often in a tank with really good plant growth you will see bubbles rising off the plant leaves. This is oxygen being produced at such a rate that it can no longer be absorbed by the water. Its only course is to escape into the atmosphere. This phenomenon is whimsically called "pearling."

Properly monitored supplemental CO_2 has no adverse effects on fish. It is a gas that is easily driven off by surface agitation. In a tank with a heavier fish population, if the pH drops below acceptable levels at night when the plants are not photosynthesizing, set an air stone on a timer when the lights are off. This easily drives off excess CO_2 and supplements the dissolved oxygen within the tank.

While it is possible to set up and maintain a planted aquarium without the use of supplemental CO_2, adding it to the water makes things easier for the aquatic gardener and allows for a much greater range of plants to be grown.

The pH/KH/CO₂ Connection

Some of the carbon dioxide (CO_2) in water forms a weak acid and, as previously noted, will lower the pH of a tank. For people with moderately hard water, this works out perfectly. Aquarists with water that has too much carbonate hardness (KH) can mix their tap water with distilled or reverse osmosis water. Anyone with very soft water must increase the carbonate hardness of the water to prevent the pH from dropping too low for the comfort of the animals in the tank.

In a tank where the supplemental CO_2 is appropriately managed, there is no lack of oxygen for the fish or other animals in the tank. In fact, because healthy, fast-growing plants produce more oxygen during photosynthesis, oxygen levels in many planted tanks can be much higher than those in the average "fish" tank. The bubbles on this *Rotala macrandra* are oxygen being produced in excess of what the water can dissolve.

The pH/KH/CO$_2$ relationship

While there are substances that can make this chart inaccurate, it is still helpful to understand the direct relationship between KH, pH, and CO$_2$. To determine the level of CO$_2$ in an aquarium, measure its pH and KH. Find the intersection of these two values in the chart. That number is the CO$_2$ level in milligrams per liter. Yellow CO$_2$ values are too high for most tanks. Blue CO$_2$ values are too low. Green CO$_2$ values indicate optimal levels.

pH

KH	6.0	6.2	6.4	6.6	6.8	7.0	7.2	7.4	7.6	7.8	8.0
0.5	15	9.3	5.9	3.7	2.4	1.5	0.9	0.6	0.4	0.2	0.15
1.0	30	18.6	11.8	7.4	4.7	3.0	1.9	1.2	0.7	0.5	0.30
1.5	44	28	17.6	11.1	7.0	4.4	2.8	1.8	1.1	0.7	0.44
2.0	59	37	24	14.8	9.4	5.9	3.7	2.4	1.5	0.9	0.59
2.5	73	48	30	18.5	11.8	7.3	4.6	3.0	2.0	1.2	0.73
3.0	87	56	35	22	14	8.7	5.6	3.5	2.2	1.4	0.87
3.5	103	65	41	26	16.4	10.3	6.5	4.1	2.6	1.6	1.03
4.0	118	75	47	30	18.7	11.8	7.5	4.7	3.0	1.9	1.18
5.0	147	93	59	37	23	14.7	9.3	5.9	3.7	2.3	1.47
6.0	177	112	71	45	28	17.7	11.2	7.1	4.5	2.8	1.77
8.0	240	149	94	59	37	24	14.9	9.4	5.9	3.7	2.4
10.0	300	186	118	74	47	30	18.6	11.8	7.4	4.7	3.0
15.0	440	280	126	111	70	44	28	17.6	11.1	7.0	4.4
20.0	590	370	240	148	94	59	37	24	14.8	9.4	5.9

Recommend increasing alkalinity by raising KH or KH + GH (general hardness)

KH

Optimal alkalinity

Water softening helpful

Too much CO$_2$ Optimal range CO$_2$ Insufficient CO$_2$

It is important to understand that pH, carbonate hardness, and CO_2 concentrations bear a direct relationship to each other, as shown in the chart on the previous page. However, this chart is accurate only if there are no other chemicals in the water (like commercial phosphate-based buffers) that cause the pH to be lower than expected. Peat and driftwood release tannins into a tank that can also lower the pH and make it appear that the CO_2 levels in the tank are actually higher than they are.

In these cases, a drop checker, which is a small glass bubble containing a solution of a known carbonate hardness plus bromothymol blue, is advisable. The bromothymol blue reacts to variations in pH by changing color. This is a better method for determining whether a tank has adequate levels of CO_2. Drop checkers range in price from a couple of dollars to $50 or more for fancier versions. Some are easier to view than others, but they all work the same way, regardless of the price.

Unfortunately, many carbonate hardness test kits give measurements in parts per million (ppm), while the pH/KH/CO_2 charts typically use the old degrees of carbonate hardness (dKH). To convert from ppm to dKH so that you can use these charts, use the following formula:

$$ppm \div 17.8 = dKH$$

To be able to safely add CO_2 to your aquarium, you need a carbonate hardness of at least 3 dKH (53 mg/L).

THE NITROGEN CYCLE

The nitrogen cycle is another one of those complicated subjects that we don't need to get into completely to understand what we need to know for the aquarium. We do need to understand the part of the cycle that goes on within an aquarium, however.

Ammonia is the first stage of the nitrogen cycle in the aquarium. Ammonia comes from fish waste, uneaten food, or fish that die and are not removed immediately. It is also present in some commercial substrates. It is toxic to fish in very small quantities, especially if the pH is above neutral (7.0).

In a heavily planted tank with good growth, it is unlikely that you will run into problems with ammonia, because the plants preferentially take up ammonia as a nitrogen source. However, if you have used a very rich substrate, or you add animals to your tank before the plants have settled in and are growing well, you could run into problems. So it is wise to check the ammonia levels in a new tank for at least the first couple of weeks.

In the second stage of the nitrogen cycle, beneficial aerobic bacteria of the genus *Nitrosomonas* will process ammonia into nitrite, which, unfortunately, is even more toxic to animals in the tank, though again, not a problem for the plants. In a newly established tank, this spike in ammonia is followed by a spike in nitrite unless the plants are growing so well that they use up all available ammonia. You want the level of nitrite to fall to zero too before introducing animals to the tank.

Finally, in the third stage, bacteria of the genera *Nitrobacter* and *Nitrospina* further break down nitrite into nitrate. In reasonable amounts, nitrate is not toxic to fish or other aquarium animals and is still a useful food for the plants. In fact, in a well-run aquarium, you will probably add nitrate to feed the plants. In tanks where nitrate is accumulating, regular water changes should deal with the build-up.

Each of these bacterial processes uses oxygen and gives off CO_2. As long as the oxygen used in the nitrogen cycle isn't significant enough to stress the fish, the CO_2 produced benefits the plants in the tank.

While the pH/KH/CO_2 chart can be helpful, a drop checker like this will give you a better idea of whether you have an adequate amount of CO_2 in your tank. If the liquid inside is blue, the CO_2 level is too low. If it is yellow, the CO_2 level is too high. If the liquid is green, the level of CO_2 is just right.

3

ESSENTIAL EQUIPMENT

PLANTED AQUARIUMS CAN BE SIMPLE, low-tech glass containers
with water and a few plants or elaborate glass tanks with sophisticated
equipment to regulate a complex natural aquatic ecosystem. In this chapter we will look
at the basic equipment choices from bare bones to the works.

TANK SIZE AND SHAPE

While it is possible to turn almost any container that holds water into an aquatic garden,
some containers definitely work better than others. If you are new to planted aquariums,
you might want to stick to a conventional aquarium shape. As you gain experience, you
can always branch out into more novel containers.

In most cases, if you are going to include fish in your aquatic garden, a traditional aquarium is a better choice. Some alternative containers can be appropriate homes for hardy
ornamental shrimp, as long as they are of a reasonable size. Very small containers can be
pretty with plants, but are not a good choice for animal occupants.

From the perspective of traditional aquascaping, the easiest ratio for producing an
attractive layout is approximately 2:1:1, where the length is twice as long as the width or
height of the tank. The commercially available tanks in the United States that most closely
approximate this shape are the 50-gallon breeder tank and the standard 75-gallon tank.
Tanks that are longer or slightly taller than this ratio can also work, but if at all possible,
avoid tanks that are shorter than this ratio in width (the back to front measurement).
Tanks that are very narrow from back to front are difficult to aquascape. Also avoid tanks
that are odd shapes, like bow fronts and hexes, especially if they are very tall, until you
have experience with traditional shapes.

An exception to the 2:1:1 ratio that is very popular, especially for desk-top sized aquariums, is cube-shaped aquariums. With a little thought, these cubes can be used effectively
to create really lovely little aquascapes.

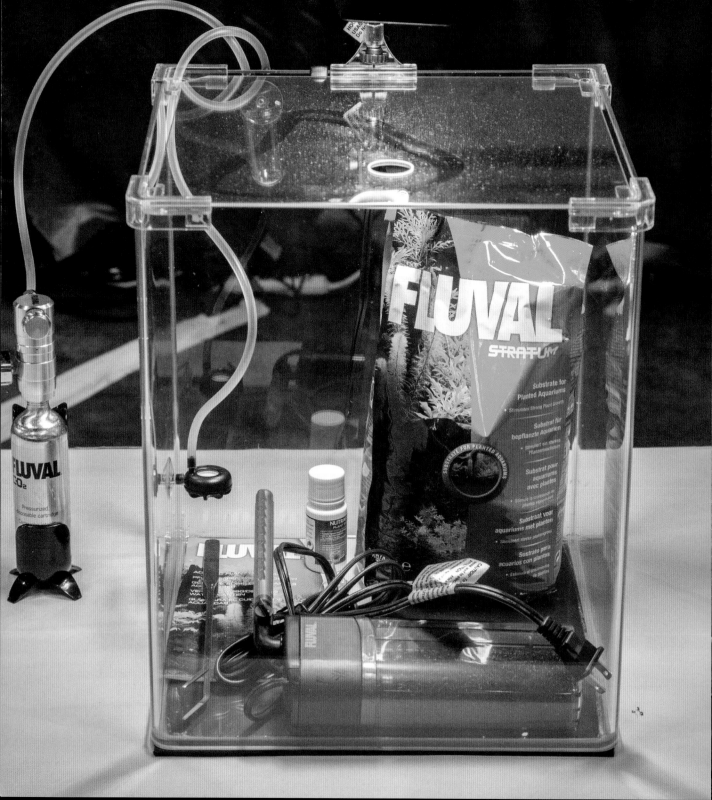

Traditional aquariums are usually made of glass, though some are made of acrylic. Acrylic tanks are more expensive than the same size glass tank and are also easily scratched. They are optically clearer than ordinary aquarium glass, but if the very slightly greenish tinge of normal aquarium glass bothers you, you can get an aquarium made of optically clear low-iron glass. Aquariums made from low-iron glass are also more expensive, but they are no more expensive than the equivalent acrylic tank, and will wear better. One advantage to acrylic tanks is, for their size, they are much lighter in weight. This can be a real consideration if you need to move a really big tank.

You can find inexpensive (and inexpensively made) aquariums at the big box pet stores. These will certainly do the job, but they tend to have poor silicone seals that are unattractive, and inexpensive plastic framing. From these low-end tanks, you can go up to progressively better-made, better-looking, more expensive tanks, some even custom made.

Today it is popular to use rimless aquariums for aquatic gardening. These give a clean, modern look to your display. Several companies make rimless tanks with nice shapes and good quality sealing work for a moderate price, but you will need to buy them from your local independent aquarium store or online.

Several companies produce kit aquariums that come with almost everything you need to get stated. These vary tremendously in quality as well as in what the kits include, so make sure you check kits out carefully, read reviews for the product you are interested in, and know exactly what you are buying.

One of the biggest variables with these kit tanks is the quality of the built-in lighting. Some tanks have plenty of light for plants, while others might be adequate for a fish-only tank, but are not strong enough to support most plant life. You may want to look for an aquarium kit made specifically as a planted or reef tank. Tanks designed for reefs often have an actinic (blue) bulb, but usually the store will be happy to switch this out for a plant-friendly bulb for you.

FILTERS

There are a number of filter options for the planted tank. In many cases, the size of the tank will make one type more suitable than another. For the very smallest tanks, which do not support animal life, you can sometimes get by with no filter at all.

Filters serve several functions in a planted tank. The first is biological filtration. In a tank stocked with fish, the filter will become colonized by nitrifying bacteria and will process the excess waste not taken up by the plants, turning it into nitrate, which is not toxic to the fish except at very high concentrations.

Another function of the filter is as a mechanical filter, straining small bits of suspended matter from the water. Not only is suspended detritus unattractive, but it is unhealthy when it settles on plant leaves and interferes with their growth.

A filter can also be filled with chemical filtration media, which removes various dissolved substances from the water. This is a less-important function in a planted tank, where the plants do much of that work for you, though there are times when certain types of chemical filtration, especially activated carbon, can be useful for short periods.

Good quality "kit" aquariums can be a great way to get started.

Most importantly in a planted tank, the filter provides water movement in the aquarium. As the pump circulates water in and out of the filter, water flows through the plant leaves, distributing CO_2 and nutrients more evenly and allowing better uptake as well. It also keeps particulate matter suspended in the water, where the filter can remove it.

A few types of filters commonly used in fish tanks are not suitable for planted tanks. These include all types of filters that are air-driven, producing a stream of air bubbles that break the water surface. Examples are bubble-up filters, air-driven sponge filters, and undergravel filters. The problem with air-driven filters is that they drive off needed CO_2 in the tank.

While water movement in the aquarium is important, avoid excess surface turbulence. Undergravel filters, even those that are not air-driven, but instead are driven by a power-head (a small water pump), are not suitable for a purposely designed planted aquarium which often uses a substrate that contains small particles. An undergravel filter stirs these particles up into the water column, making a horrible mess.

I would also stay away from internal power filters, even though they come with some with kit aquariums, because they are hard to hide in the tank, and it can be disruptive getting the filter in and out of the tank for cleaning. Anything that makes a filter hard to clean will make it likely that maintenance will be neglected.

Hang-on-the-back filters are appropriate for small aquariums like this 4-gallon tank.

48

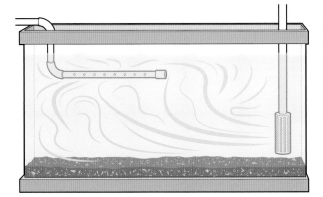

When the intake and return ends of a filter are placed on opposite ends of a tank, water flow is chaotic. ◄

When the intake and return are placed on the same end, with the intake at the bottom of the tank and the return at the top, optimal water flow is achieved. ►

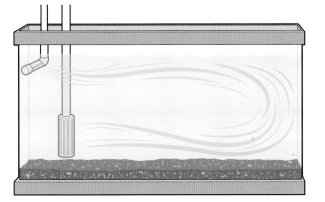

For an extremely large tank, like this one belonging to my late friend, Steen Jansen in Thailand, a sump-style filter is really the only viable option. ▼

For tanks of 20 gallons or less, external, hang-on-the-back overflow-style filters are the most common choice, though there are nice, small canister filters available for small tanks now too. Hang-on tank filters suck water up out of the tank, move it through the filtration media, and then return it to the tank. These filters are inexpensive and the better brands are very reliable.

I prefer the type of hang-on filter that uses a sponge block as the main filtration media. It is both a good mechanical filter and a good biological filter. The sponge block can be squeezed clean in running water and used over and over, almost indefinitely. Other filters have disposable cartridges that must be purchased and replaced regularly. Not only does this get expensive, but I prefer to put as little waste into our landfills as possible.

Mid-size and larger planted aquariums are most often run with canister filters.

For larger tanks, most aquatic gardeners choose canister filters. Such filters keep most of the equipment out of the tank and in the cabinet below. The only pieces of equipment in the tank are the intake and return tubes. The best flow can be achieved with a canister filter if the intake tube is placed low down on one end of the tank, and the return spray bar placed high in the tank on the same end, set to send water flow across the top of the tank from one end to the other, returning to the intake in a circular pattern.

For the largest tanks, an overflow, sump-style filter is often the best choice. These filters require a little more knowledge to install than other types but they have the largest capacity and they allow the aquarist to remove all equipment from the tank. Since this book is an introduction to aquatic gardening and few people will choose to start with a tank requiring a sump-style filter, I won't go into depth about them here.

HEATERS—DO YOU NEED THEM?

If you go into a pet store asking for an aquarium set-up, you will invariably be sold a heater along with the package. Whether you need one or not in a planted tank depends on a number of variables. If your aquarium is in the living area of your house and you maintain normal household temperatures, you may not need a heater. The equipment used to run your tank gives off heat and will keep the tank warmer than ambient temperature during the day. At night, the tank will cool down, but this happens in shallow water in the wild too, and many fish tolerate the drop in temperature without any trouble.

Some fish such as rams (*Microgeophagus ramerizi*) or discus (*Symphysodon discus*) and the often poorly treated heat-loving Siamese fighting fish (*Betta splendens*) must be kept at warmer temperatures (78°–82°F) to remain healthy. Another exception is a very small tank that is 10 gallons or less. Such a tank does not have enough mass to hold heat during the cooler evening hours and will need a heater if it contains tropical fish.

Discus require warm temperatures, so in most climates that means that the tank will need a heater. Aquascape by Filipe Olivera.

If you choose to use a heater, a fully submersible or inline, thermostatically adjustable heater is preferred. Such a heat source is not only easier to hide, but it also tends to be more reliable. Make sure that you choose a heater that is properly sized for your aquarium. When heaters fail, it is often because they remain stuck in the on position. If you use a large heater in a small tank, you can easily kill all your fish before you notice it.

In older literature about planted tanks, you may come across mention of heating cables that were buried in the substrate. In fact, they can still be purchased from at least one vendor. Many years of experience have now taught us that substrate heating does not yield better growth than other methods in most circumstances.

What is important, however, is that the substrate does not become significantly colder than the rest of the tank. This can happen if the tank is placed in a very cool part of the house, like a poorly heated basement. A glass-bottomed tank placed on an open wrought iron stand is particularly susceptible becoming too cold.

An easy way to solve the problem is to tape a sheet of florists' foam to the bottom of the tank for insulation. Likewise, if the aquarium must be placed near a window, tape the sheet of foam on the side toward the window to protect the tank from both excess light and heat.

LIGHTING

In nature, sunlight drives plant growth and photosynthesis. In the aquatic garden, artificial light sources are needed to make sure plants receive an adequate amount of light.

The amount of light that an aquascape requires depends on the types of plants grown in it. Just as with terrestrial plants, there are shade plants for aquariums, sun plants, and many plants that tolerate both conditions. Since plants that need high light conditions also need more CO_2, more nutrient supplementation, and more trimming, aquatic gardeners who prefer less maintenance often choose a lower light/slower growth system. The trade-off is that many beautiful plants cannot be maintained without stronger light levels.

It is important to understand that light is the engine that drives everything that happens in a tank. Just as a small economy car can run quite effectively with a small engine that requires much less fuel, a large car requires a bigger engine and more fuel to perform at the same level. Or, you can have a small, high-performance sports car with a big engine that requires lots of premium gasoline, specialized tires, and so on. This sports car may be shiny and exciting, but it is going to be more expensive to run and it will require more maintenance. It's all a matter of balance.

You can have an easy, fun, slow-growth aquarium with lower light levels, or a stunning sports car model requiring daily dosing and frequent maintenance. The choice is yours, and the light you choose will be the deciding factor in how you manage many other aspects of your aquarium.

Light Qualities

Lighting has several important aspects, and some that are often discussed are not important at all. Before looking at the pros and cons of various types of aquarium lighting, we need to define a few terms.

A watt is a measure of electricity used, not light produced. An old incandescent bulb uses more watts of electricity than a fluorescent tube, which still uses more electricity than LEDs to produce the same amount of light.

Watts per gallon (WPG) provided a useful rule of thumb back when the typical aquarium lighting was normal output fluorescents over traditionally shaped fish tanks. This measurement has never been useful with tanks that are unusual shapes, and it goes right out the window when using high output fluorescents and LED fixtures.

Color rendering index (CRI) is a measure of how natural things look under a certain type of light. Think of how things look under sodium-vapor street lights—all yellowish and washed out. Sodium-vapor lamps produce a lot of light for the amount of input energy (which makes them good street lights), but they have a terrible CRI. While CRI doesn't affect how plants grow under a particular lamp, CRI is important to people, because we want to enjoy the look of our beautiful planted tanks.

Kelvin (K) units rate the color temperature of a lamp. Noon-day light is between 5,000 and 6,500K. Cooler temperature lamps, from 7,500 to 10,000K, look more bluish to our eyes, while warmer temperature lamps, below 5,000K, look more yellowish. This tells you nothing about how the lamps will grow plants, but you may have a preference in terms of what color of light appeals to your eyes.

Lumens and lux are two measures that really confuse people, because they seem to say something about the brightness of various light sources. They do, but they only measure those parts of the spectrum that are visible to the human eye. Since this is the part of the spectrum that plants use the least effectively, lumens and lux are not particularly useful measures of how a specific lamp will grow plants in an aquarium.

Spectral curve is where we get into things that are important to plants. Plants can use a much larger area of the light spectrum than humans can see. People see mostly in the green area of the spectrum, while red and blue light are very important to some aspects of plant growth. This does not mean that plants can't also use light in the green part of the spectrum; they just don't use it as efficiently. And if some red and blue light is not available,

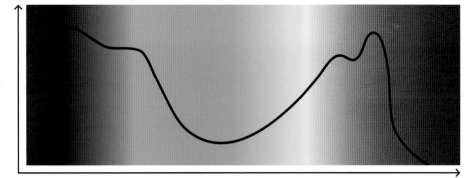

Rate of photosynthesis
(%)

Wavelength (nanometers)

Plants utilize red and blue light
more efficiently than green
light for photosynthesis.

you can get some strange growth responses. Spectral charts are available for many of the lamps currently on the market. While these are not usually included in the packaging, they are often available from the manufacturer, either on their Web site, or for the asking.

Most modern fluorescent bulbs, even cheap ones from home improvement stores, are tri-phosphor tubes. Such lights have been coated with three different phosphors that luminesce in different ranges of the spectrum—red, green, and blue. This makes them a good choice for plant growth and, at the same time, pleasing to the human eye.

Photosynthetically Active Radiation

Photosynthetically active radiation (PAR) is the only measure that tells us anything useful about how a particular light source will grow plants. A simplistic explanation of PAR is that it measures radiation in the part of the spectrum that can be used by photosynthetic life forms. The units of measure for PAR are μmols (micromoles per square meter per second), that is, the number of photons in the parts of the spectrum that plants can use that hit a square meter per second. Aquarists often use the term PAR as short-hand for μmols in conversation.

In nature, the amount of light reaching plants in a body of water depends on weather, time of day, time of year, turbidity, water color and depth. Many plants tolerate a wide range of lighting conditions as long as their other needs are properly met. In the wild, in strong midday sun in the tropics, the PAR in clear shallow water is often well over 1000 μmols. Earlier and later in the day, this number is lower. At 8:30 in the morning when the sun is at a strong angle, I have measured PAR at 130 μmols in 5 cm of very clear water.

The author measuring PAR in the wild. This water was clear, but strongly colored with tannins. This reduces the amount of light reaching the plants.

Although this is still more light than most of people provide to their aquariums, it shows the tremendous range of PAR in the course of the day in the wild.

In the aquarium, we can use lower levels of light, with a more consistent intensity during the day. There is no clear agreement on what light levels are considered low, medium, and high in the planted aquarium. I find that light levels below 25–30 PAR (which is the way you will often see these numbers recorded in aquarium literature) are low enough that planted aquariums can get by without supplemental CO_2, though even at this level, the plants would benefit from it.

Light levels from 30 to 50 PAR are in the medium range. At this level, some people might choose not to use supplemental CO_2, but their plants would grow better and their aquariums would have fewer problems with algae if they did supplement with CO_2.

Above 50 PAR, in what I call high light, plants quickly exhaust the CO_2 available within the tank unless it is supplemented. Under these light conditions, without supplemental CO_2, the tank is likely to experience significant algae problems. Some people, especially those who are experienced aquatic gardeners and have an interest in species that demand high light, run their tanks with much higher light levels, but most of the plants that a novice aquatic gardener is likely to encounter can be grown successfully at 50 PAR or a bit more as long as adequate CO_2 and other nutrients are available.

A PAR meter can be purchased on the internet or through certain hydroponics supply stores. A good quality, commercially made PAR meter will cost about $300; however, a few individuals are making low-cost PAR meters that are available via the internet for $50 to $100. The homemade meters have limitations if used outdoors, but are reliable enough for home aquarium use.

Another option for a home aquarist is to join a local aquarium or aquatic gardening club. Many of these groups have a PAR meter that belongs to the club and can be borrowed or rented by individual members for a small fee. You can, of course, be successful with planted aquariums without using a PAR meter, but you will have to depend on your local aquarium store to help you choose appropriate light levels for your tank. In a case like this, it makes sense to be sure that the person giving the advice actually has planted tank experience. Look at the planted tanks in the store. Do they look good? If so, you can probably get good advice there.

You cannot make up for lack of light intensity with increased duration, though with extremely bright light you may sometimes need to limit duration to avoid algae problems. In general, the lights should be illuminating your planted tank for 6 to 10 hours per day. Put the lights on a timer so you don't need to remember to turn them on and off.

Some people use lights on different timers so they can have a shorter period of very bright light in the middle of the day, with periods of lower intensity earlier and later. Others who really enjoy tinkering with technology choose to use electronic dimmers that mimic the changing intensity as the sun rises and falls each day. Reproducing a full daylight cycle may be fun but for most aquatic gardeners, especially if you are just starting out, this is not necessary. It is also fine to break your photoperiod into two shorter periods if it helps you enjoy your aquarium around your work day.

Normal Output Fluorescent Lighting

We live in a time when there are a number of good options for lighting the planted tank. Not that long ago the only reasonable option was the old-style standard output fluorescent. The width of these tubes made it difficult to get enough light over the top of the tank, so it was almost impossible to get too much light over the tank. Now we have a number of different options for lighting and we have to be careful about both underlighting and overlighting the tank.

Modern, normal output fluorescent tubes come in two types based on their widths. T8 tubes are 1 inch in diameter, while T5 tubes are 5/8 inch in diameter. T5s are more efficient than T8s, but they are also more costly. T8s are the current standard for shop lights purchased at home improvement stores. As such, they are a very inexpensive way to light tanks that are the right size (4-foot-long tanks in particular).

The problem with fluorescent lights is that at least half of the light is sent up into the fixture away from the surface of the tank. This means that the better your reflector is the more light that will bounce back into the tank.

The best reflectors have mirror surface and parabolic shape. When you look into the fixture, you can clearly see not only the tubes, but their reflections as well. A reflector of this quality will give you a much greater amount of light then a poor-quality reflector. This is part of the reason that T5s are more efficient than T8s. The thinner bulbs block less of the reflected light from reaching the tank than thicker ones do.

T5 High Output Fluorescent Lighting

T5 high output (T5 HO) lighting is the state-of-the-art in fluorescent lighting for the planted aquarium. They put out substantially more light than normal output fluorescents. The fixtures are reasonably priced and replacement bulbs are not terribly expensive.

However, many aquarium trade fixtures have poor ballasts, and the lights are too close together, causing heat to build up. As a result, the light level of the bulbs in these poorly designed fixtures degrades, and the bulbs must be replaced fairly frequently and long before they actually burn out.

In good-quality fixtures with good ballasts and adequate air flow around the lights to keep them from overheating, the bulbs should last about a year. If the fixtures run hot or if poor-quality ballasts are used, the light levels may degrade much faster.

Like normal output and compact fluorescents, the amount of light that actually reaches your tank is also very dependent on the quality of the reflector. Quality T5 high output fixtures are a good choice for most traditionally shaped aquariums, and typically give enough light to grow a wide selection of plants.

Compact Fluorescent Lighting

Compact fluorescent (CF) lighting is essentially a T5 high output tube that is bent to fit more light in a smaller space. The CFs typically used over aquariums are U-shaped. These can be a very useful form of lighting for fitting tank shapes other than the traditional 4-foot-long rectangular tank, but as with other forms of fluorescent lighting, their efficiency is very much dependent on the quality of the reflector.

The U-shaped CFs typically used in aquarium fixtures can be a very attractive option for a moderately lit tank. They may not have enough intensity to support high light foreground plants in deeper tanks, but they maintain their intensity well over an extended time. If they are properly ventilated, good-quality CFs are still producing 80 percent of their original light levels at the end of their life.

The spiral type CFs in many household applications are sometimes used by do-it-yourselfer aquarists, because they are inexpensive to purchase and readily available. But their light production is hampered by their shape, and it is hard to find reflectors that substantially help this situation. In the long run, spiral-shaped CFs are not a great choice for the planted aquarium. Though they can be used to grow plants in the low light category, there are more efficient ways of doing this.

Metal Halide Lighting

Metal halides have been a popular choice for reef tank keepers for many years, and they are also an occasional choice for aquatic gardeners. They are roughly as efficient as normal output T5s. The big difference is that while a fluorescent tube spreads light over the length of the tank, a metal halide concentrates the light in a small area. To cover the whole footprint of the tank, you must either raise the light higher above the water surface or add more lights. Practically speaking, the only option when using metal halides on a smaller tank is to raise or lower the fixture to regulate the amount of light.

Normal output T8 fluorescents can give very nice growth in a tank with the right types of plants. ▲

Compact fluorescents fit a wide range of tank sizes and put out a lot of light. ▶

Metal halide lighting has plenty of intensity but is not without its challenges. Notice the "hot spots" of brightest light. Aquascape by Steve Wilson.

Metal halides produce very good, strong lighting that can grow just about any aquatic plant, but this light source also has its downside. The fixtures and replacement bulbs are both expensive, and as the bulbs age, there can be some fairly significant color shifts. This means that if you replace one bulb at a time (as they burn out), parts of the tank can look very different than other parts.

Metal halides also produce quite a bit of concentrated heat. If they are used in a closed canopy, you must also plan some kind of ventilation, preferably in the form of fans, to keep air circulating around them. It is also possible to use metal halides in pendants over an open-topped tank, which solves the problem of heat build-up, but results in quite a bit of very bright light spilling into the room, which may be objectionable in the living area of the house.

LED Lighting

The wave of the future in lighting in all sorts of applications is light emitting diodes (LEDs). Almost everyone these days has had some contact with this form of lighting, whether in a small, bright flashlight or in the tail lights of a newer car. At the time this book is being written, LED aquarium lighting is coming of age. Most beginner aquarium kits sold at the big box stores come with some form of LED lighting. It is still expensive to light a larger aquarium with good quality LEDs, but the cost has dropped dramatically in the last few years, and the trend is sure to continue.

LED lighting is made up of many tiny little individual lights, or diodes. These come in a number of different colors, which can be mixed together to achieve the desired spectrum. When you choose LED fixtures, keep in mind the needs of your plants. It is fine to include green or white bulbs so that the light looks good to your eyes (otherwise, why have an aquatic garden in your home?), but also include red and blue lights for the plants.

LED fixtures are the most energy efficient form of lighting currently available. The individual lights are long lasting, and losing one or two doesn't significantly reduce the light output of the fixture.

Andrey Kalinin's do-it-yourself LED lights and tank. ▶

The best LEDs for our purposes will include red and blue diodes for the plants and green and white diodes for good viewing quality. This light strip has been turned way down so that you can see the colors. When it is turned up, it is extremely bright, and to our eyes, it looks like a white light source. ▼

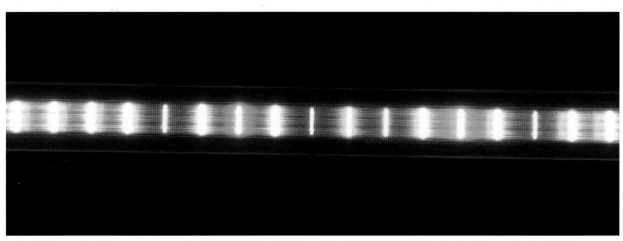

Another nice attribute of LEDs is that many of them can be used with either a manual or electronic dimmer switch. This feature can be very handy for lowering light levels if you are experiencing algae problems in a tank. Or you can get fancy with a digital controller and have them run in a full daytime sequence, slowly increasing in intensity in the morning and decreasing through a twilight period in the evening.

As manufacturers become more familiar with the needs of aquatic gardeners, more of them are producing fixtures specifically targeted for this audience. There are even specialty manufacturers who will build beautiful custom fixtures for a tank (an ideal but expensive option). Be careful though, as many commercially available fixtures are designed for fish-only or reef tanks. Those for fish tanks do not have the intensity to grow plants other than the most shade tolerant of plants. Those designed for reef tanks do not have the light spectrum preferred for a planted tank (though some people are using them successfully).

Another option for those who are handy is to put together your own LED lighting. This can be done quite inexpensively either starting from scratch or using one of several modular systems with less assembly required.

Another consideration with LED lighting is that the lights tend not to have much spread compared with fluorescent lighting. Because of this, except on the smallest tanks, it is likely that you will need more than one strip of LEDs to effectively light the tank. Some high-end manufacturers can also customize the spread of the lights by using individual lenses or optics, which concentrate the light into a cone. The cone can have an angle of 100 degrees, 90 degrees, or even smaller to reduce or increase the spread of light. For instance, a strip with 90-degree lenses spreads the light further than one set at 70 degrees. When purchasing ready-made commercial LED fixtures, you will get more even coverage by looking for those where the lenses give a spread of 90 to 100 degrees.

Diffuse vs. Point Source Lighting

When choosing a lighting system for your tank, it is important to think about whether you will be using diffuse light with more coverage, like fluorescent lighting, or point source lighting, like metal halides or LEDs, which can reach deeper into the tank but cover less of the tank's footprint. Both types of systems can be used successfully, but will dictate how much lighting you have available, where you place the fixture on the tank, what plants you use, and where you place them.

For instance, if you have a 75-gallon tank (approximately 4 feet long, 18 inches from back to front, and about 18 inches to the substrate surface), you might choose a T5 high output quad fixture and place it over the middle of the tank. This would give you very good light in the middle of the tank. The taller plants that are typically placed in the rear of the tank will be closer to the light because of their height, so you would probably have enough light for very good growth in that area of the tank as well. However, you might find that there is enough light fall-off at the front of the tank that foreground plants requiring high light would struggle.

If you were to choose metal halide lighting for such a tank, a single fixture would give you a very bright area in the middle with much less light on the ends. Two metal halides would be extremely high light over this size tank, and you would probably have to raise them up to reduce the intensity.

A single strip-type LED fixture would not be capable of producing enough spread for good growth in a tank of this size from back to front, so you could choose to use two strips, one placed toward the back of the tank, the other toward the front. With good-quality fixtures of adequate spectrum, this should give you quite good lighting, easily allowing growth of high light foreground plants, and giving plenty of light to light-loving stem plants in the back. You would have an area of lower intensity in the middle, however, and could plan on using this area for hardscape materials and more shade tolerant species.

Light Intensity in Open-topped and Covered Aquariums

Finally, we need to consider other problems that can affect the light reaching your plants. Obviously, floating plants can reduce the amount of light reaching the plants below significantly. Discolored water, suspended particulate matter, and surface film can also cut light levels significantly so it is important to keep the aquarium clean. Even a very clean cover glass will cut light intensity by about 20 percent, so if you use one, keep your cover glass as clean as possible.

Because of the problems with glass covers, many people choose to keep their planted aquariums open topped, without any cover. The advantages are, of course, that more light can enter the tank and you have the opportunity to quickly and easily access the tank to tweak "just one little thing" as you walk by. One of the disadvantages is that an open top significantly reduces fish choices, because many species will jump out of an open-topped tank. The other big disadvantage is that you will have to regularly top up the tank to make up for evaporation.

Either option can work; it's up to you to choose which you prefer and to plan your lights accordingly. It is equally important to keep the walls of the tank very clean, inside and out. Clean glass is reflective, and will bounce light back into your tank to help your plants.

LEDs are the lighting of the future . . . until the next big breakthrough comes along. Because LEDs don't have the spread that some other light sources do, you may need more than one strip to light your tank adequately.

CARBON DIOXIDE SYSTEMS

It is possible to have an attractive planted aquarium without using supplemental carbon dioxide (CO_2), but you must plan it carefully. The light level must be low enough that it doesn't drive plants into CO_2 deprivation. At the same time, you need to plan where the CO_2 for the plants will come from. (They still need some, they will just need less.)

Obviously, there is some CO_2 in the atmosphere all the time, and some of it dissolves in the aquarium too, but it is a very small amount. Room air contains 1–3 mg/L of CO_2, and aerated water dissolves only about 70 percent of that CO_2. This amount is not nearly enough to sustain growth of even low light plants.

Fortunately, the respiration of the fish and plants along with the biological activity in the filter and the substrate produce CO_2 that can be available to plants if it is not driven off by excess surface agitation. If you choose to try a tank without supplemental CO_2, make sure that you choose a filtration system that does not unnecessarily agitate the water surface. This means no air-driven filters can be used and that the return of power filters should be below the surface of the water if at all possible.

The no (supplemental) CO_2 option can be a viable one as long as you choose slow-growth plants and keep the light level low as well.

Low-tech Yeast Reactor

For those who would like to see the benefits of supplemental CO_2, but who are not ready to take the leap into pressurized CO_2, a simple yeast reactor might be a comfortable starting point. There are several companies that manufacture yeast reactor kits. They are relatively inexpensive and provide all the pieces you need in a nice, neat box. But it is also quite easy to make your own yeast reactor.

All you need to set up a simple yeast reactor is an empty plastic bottle, some airline tubing, a nail, pliers, yeast, and some sugar. I prefer 2-liter juice bottles because they are more rigid than soda pop bottles and don't collapse if squeezed a little too hard.

Holding the nail with the pliers, heat the nail on the stove until it is hot enough to melt through the bottle top. Make a hole in the bottle top just slightly smaller than the diameter of your airline tubing. When the plastic has cooled, cut the end of the airline tubing at an angle, so that you have a pointed end to stick through the hole in the bottle top. Use the pliers to pull the tubing through so that you have at least 1 inch of tubing inside the bottle. If you have made the hole slightly smaller than the tubing, it will make an air-tight seal without the use of any glue.

Fill the bottle half-way to two-thirds full with tepid water. Do not use hot water, which will kill the yeast. Using a funnel, pour 1 cup of sugar and ¼ teaspoon of yeast into the bottle and swirl the bottle around to mix well. Make sure you don't fill the bottle too full. The mixture may foam, and you don't want that getting into your aquarium. Screw the cap on the bottle and attach the other end of the tubing to a CO_2 diffuser. Alternatively, place the tubing into the intake of a filter or powerhead.

Place the bottle on top of the aquarium until you see it start producing bubbles. Once the CO_2 gas begins to produce positive pressure in the tubing, you can place the bottle below the aquarium if you choose. However, it is still safest to use a check valve to prevent any backflow.

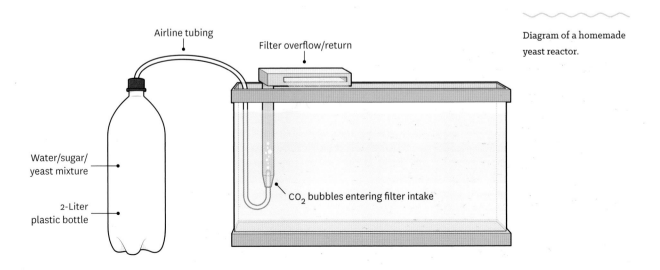

Airline tubing

Filter overflow/return

Water/sugar/
yeast mixture

2-Liter
plastic bottle

CO_2 bubbles entering filter intake

Diagram of a homemade
yeast reactor.

A yeast reactor typically produces CO_2 for two to four weeks as the yeast converts the sugar to alcohol. Eventually, the level of alcohol in the bottle kills the active yeast. The CO_2 production dwindles and eventually stops. CO_2 production can be evened out and lengthened by using yeast designed to withstand higher alcohol levels, like that used in making beer and wine. If your tap water is very soft, add a small amount of baking soda to the mix to even CO_2 production out more.

A yeast reactor system can produce enough CO_2 for a moderately lit small tank (up to about 15 gallons) if the aquarist is diligent about maintaining the culture and changing the mixture as needed. Some people with larger tanks use two (or more) yeast reactors, and change them on a staggered schedule to maintain as even a supply of CO_2 as possible to the tank.

Never put a shut off valve of any kind on a yeast reactor system. If CO_2 is not allowed to flow freely from the bottle, the build-up of pressure could cause the bottle to explode, making a sticky, smelly mess.

While yeast reactors are a reasonable way to learn about the benefits of CO_2, most people find the maintenance becomes a chore, and they don't like dealing with the smelly liquid left in the bottles when CO_2 production ceases. Very few serious aquatic gardeners stick with yeast reactors long-term.

Low-tech Citric Acid Reactor

A second, less common, but very useful type of low-tech CO_2 supplementation uses two pop bottles, one with baking soda, and the other with either citric acid or vinegar. The bottles are attached to a small, pre-made unit that includes a needle valve, a pressure relief valve, and tubing to go from bottle to bottle and from the unit to the aquarium.

This system works by dripping tiny amounts of citric acid (or vinegar) into the bottle with the baking soda and water mix. The two compounds release CO_2, which is then pumped, under pressure, into the aquarium. The system produces a steady stream of CO_2, delivered at a constant rate, for several weeks. How long it lasts, of course, depends on the size of the tank, and the targeted rate of CO_2 diffusion.

I find this system, which is relatively new to the hobby, to be much superior to a yeast reactor, both in terms of rate of production and steady supply and it is only a little bit more expensive. So far, these systems are only being produced in the Far East, and are sold on eBay.

Pressurized Gas Options

Sooner or later, most serious aquatic gardeners choose to use pressurized gas for supplemental CO_2. With a reliable regulator and needle valve, and an efficient method of diffusing CO_2 into the aquarium, pressurized gas is the easiest and, in the long run, most economical way to deliver a reliable flow of CO_2 to the aquarium.

Cylinder size and weight. A few manufacturers of very small pressurized CO_2 systems rely on small paintball-type cartridges. Most of these cartridges are nonrefillable, though they can and should be recycled. Some of these systems come with passive diffusion "bells"

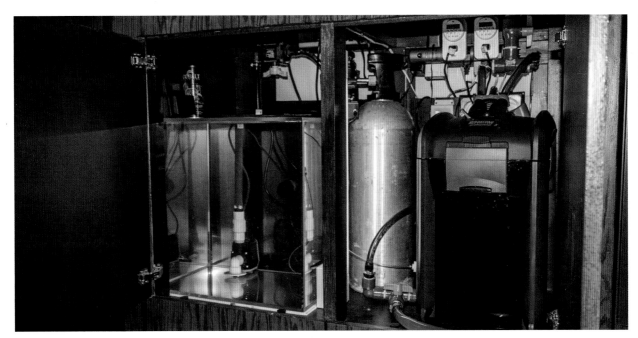

Pressurized CO_2 system under a tank.

that are filled daily by the user and slowly diffuse into the water column. This is, perhaps, better than nothing, but you cannot get significant CO_2 levels out of a bell diffusion system. I advise against this method.

The next step up still uses paintball cartridges, but has a small regulator and bubble counter, and feeds into a glass diffuser inside the aquarium. These systems tend to be finicky and require careful monitoring to maintain an even flow, but they can provide adequate amounts of CO_2 for tanks up to about 10 gallons. The biggest problem is that the paintball cartridges don't hold much CO_2, so you find yourself in an endless loop of purchasing expensive replacements. There are, however, also small refillable paintball CO_2 cylinders and regulators of sufficient size for nano tanks. These are not significantly less expensive than the full-sized versions, but they can be an attractive option for someone short on space.

With a tank of any size, or if your interests are in growing a wide variety of more demanding plants, a regular CO_2 cylinder from a local gas supply store is the way to go. These cylinders are available in a variety of sizes. My personal preference is for 5-pound cylinders for two reasons. First, they are lightweight enough to carry around easily, and second, they can be hidden inside almost any aquarium cabinet. Remember that the "5-pound" rating is for the amount of CO_2 the cylinder will hold, not the weight of the cylinder itself. To hold gas under pressure, these cylinders themselves are quite heavy, so the actual weight will be significantly more than 5 pounds, especially when full.

There are other sizes, though, if you prefer. People who run a number of aquariums off the same CO_2 cylinder often opt for a 20-pound cylinder. These are both bulky and heavy, but all carbon dioxide tanks in the United States, regardless of size, other than the paintball cylinders and cartridges, are threaded for the same regulators.

Purchasing or renting cylinders. Depending on where you live, there may be options to purchase a tank or rent one. Where I live, the most common arrangement is that you purchase the initial tank, but every time you go in for a refill, you trade the empty tank for a full one. The advantage of this arrangement is that you never have to worry about your tank getting too old and unsafe. Every tank has a hydro test date on it and must be periodically inspected. If it doesn't pass this inspection, it can no longer be used. If you own the tank outright, it will be your responsibility to replace it. If your gas company has either a rental or trade-in policy, they are the ones who deal with tanks that can no longer be safely used.

Handling cylinders safely. While CO_2 cylinders are very safe if handled properly, it is important to follow some simple safety rules with them. The gas in these bottles is, of course, nonflammable, but it is under tremendous pressure. Because of this it is very important that the cylinders not be placed in a position where they can be knocked over either while in use or while being transported. If the valve on the top were to be knocked off, the cylinder could become an unguided missile. Likewise, full cylinders should not be left in a closed up hot car, as this could cause them to explode.

Finally, when the canister is attached to your regulator, the valve open, and you are ready to operate the system, the canister must be in an upright position. In that position, only the gaseous CO_2 at the top of the tank will come into contact with the regulator. If the tank is laying on its side, the pressurized liquid CO_2 inside could get into the regulator and ruin it. If you have children in the house, it is very important to make sure that they do not have access to your pressurized CO_2 equipment. Make sure it is secured in the cabinet beneath the aquarium with a childproof lock.

Choosing a regulator. To get the CO_2 gas from the tank to the aquarium, you will need several pieces of equipment. The first is a good quality regulator. This is not a place to go cheap. Poor quality regulators often have an end-of-tank dump, when the pressure in the tank starts to decrease. This defect causes the tank to release all the remaining CO_2 into the aquarium at the same time. The results are often catastrophic—killing all the animals in the tank. Good quality regulators are more expensive, but control the CO_2 until the cylinder is empty.

While it is possible to find all the separate parts needed to put a CO_2 system together on your own, most people prefer to buy an all-in-one unit. These consist of the regulator, a needle valve that further reduces the flow to the tiny amounts wanted to introduce into the aquarium, a bubble counter that allows a quick "eyeball" check of the flow of CO_2, and a solenoid.

The solenoid is a device that automatically turns off the flow of CO_2 when the lights aren't on. A solenoid is not an absolute necessity, unless you have very soft water or you run very high CO_2 levels, but it will save you trips for CO_2 refills by limiting CO_2 dosing to those hours when the plants are photosynthesizing.

A few specialized aquarium shops carry CO_2 equipment, but many people may find they need to order this equipment online.

Connecting the cylinder to the aquarium. The next step is to attach the regulator and cylinder to the aquarium. It is best to use CO_2-resistant tubing for this, as it will last the longest without becoming brittle. If such tubing is not available, regular airline tubing

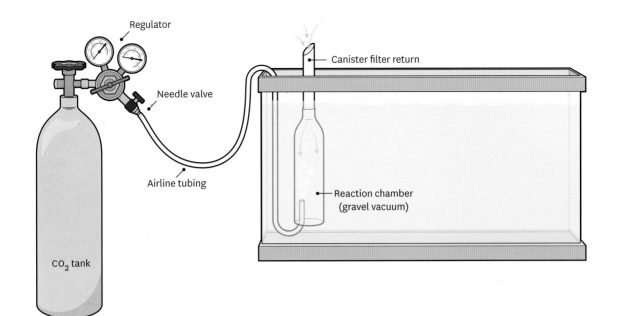

Regulator

Canister filter return

Needle valve

Airline tubing

Reaction chamber
(gravel vacuum)

CO_2 tank

Diagram of a homemade semi-automatic CO_2 system.

from aquarium shops will also do. Just remember that airline tubing will get brittle with age and need to be replaced.

Please use a CO_2-resistant check valve between the aquarium and the regulator. This will prevent water from inadvertently backing up into your expensive CO_2 equipment.

Getting carbon dioxide into the aquarium. Finally, you will need a way to dissolve the CO_2 into your aquarium water. CO_2 actually dissolves easily in water as long as there is a good amount of contact.

There are two main methods of dissolving CO_2 into the water. The simplest and most suitable to small tanks is a CO_2 diffuser. This is a small disk that is attached to the end of the tubing, and, usually with a suction cup, attached to the wall of the aquarium. The disk breaks the CO_2 into microscopic bubbles, which dissolve as they rise through the water. It is important to place the diffuser as low in the aquarium as possible to allow for the longest period of contact.

Some diffusers work with low pressure CO_2, like that from a yeast reactor, but others must have considerable pressure behind them to work. Make sure you purchase one that is appropriate for the type of CO_2 system you have chosen.

The second option is a CO_2 reactor, which uses moving water to tumble with the CO_2 bubbles and dissolve them. This type of system dissolves more gas more quickly and efficiently than a diffuser, so is a better choice for a larger aquarium. Some reactors are driven by a powerhead and sit inside the aquarium or inside a sump-style filter chamber. Others are inserted in the return line from a canister filter. Any of these options can work well. It is really up to the choice of the aquatic gardener.

4

SUBSTRATES

UBSTRATES FOR PLANTED AQUARIUMS fall into one of three categories, each with its pros and cons. First are a variety of commercial products, some of which are more suitable for fish than plants, but others are designed specifically for plants. In the second category are gravel and amended gravel substrates. Third are soil and several nontraditional substrates. Which type of substrate you choose depends on what you intend to put into your aquarium.

COMMERCIAL COMPLETE SUBSTRATES

Commercial aquarium gravel that is coated or colored is completely unsuitable for plant growth. It has no nutritional value and the coating makes it difficult for plant roots to grab hold of the gravel. However, a wide range of substrates can be used in a planted tank, ranging from inert gravel to soil substrates.

A number of good commercial soil-based products are available today. These are typically pressed into very small pellets, and the bag will have a distinct "potting soil" smell when you open it. These provide nutrients to the plants through at least the first few months. The best provide some level of nutrition through the first year or two.

A tank with a modern, commercial soil-based substrate.

In a low to moderately lit tank, a commercial soil-based substrate may provide enough nutrients to support plant growth without any supplementation for a long time. However, most people find that in a higher light, fast-growth set-up they need to feed their plants, starting within the first couple of months, even with a nutritious substrate. For someone starting with planted tanks, I strongly advise using one of these commercial substrate mixes. They help you provide for your plants while you are learning and won't cause the mess some do-it-yourself substrates can.

COMMERCIAL CALCINED CLAY SUBSTRATES

Another option is a commercial calcined clay substrate. This type of substrate has little built-in nutritional value, but is very porous and has the ability to capture and hold nutrients. The ability of a substrate to take up and store nutrients is called cation exchange capacity (CEC). If a substrate has a high CEC, it will grab some of the nutrients out of the water column and hold them in reserve. The plant roots are then able to access these nutrients.

The porous nature of these substrates also makes it easier for plants to grab hold of them. These attributes make this type of substrate a better choice than plain quartz aquarium gravel, but you will need to dose nutrients through the water column almost immediately except in the very lowest light, slow-growth tanks. Commercial calcined clay products range in color from reddish brown to black.

GRAVEL AND AMENDED GRAVEL SUBSTRATES

It is possible to grow some aquatic plants in plain, inert aquarium gravel, pool filter sand, or traction sand that is between 1 and 3 mm in diameter. The downside is that until mulm (detritus from the plants and fish) starts to build up in the substrate, the plants are entirely dependent on you to meet all their nutritional needs through the water column. This can be a tall order for a novice aquatic gardener.

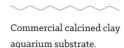

Commercial calcined clay aquarium substrate.

It is also possible to use a mostly gravel substrate and amend it with various materials so that it becomes a better medium for your plants. Besides a lack of nutrients, the other problem with plain, inert substrates like quartz sand is that they can't grab hold of nutrients and store them for the plants' later use.

Plain quartz gravel has a very low cation exchange capacity. One way to significantly improve it is to mix laterite, an iron-bearing red clay from tropical regions, into the bottom layer of the substrate, and cap it with a layer of clean gravel. Laterite is available commercially. It is even more effective if a handful of peat moss is mixed in. The peat moss keeps the pH in the substrate lower and allows the plants to access nutrients more easily. In the early days of aquatic gardening, this was one of the most common methods of setting up a substrate. Today many better choices exist, but it is still possible to have a beautiful and long-term aquatic garden using this method.

HOMEMADE SOIL-BASED AND NONTRADITIONAL SUBSTRATES

While I do not recommend soil or nontraditional substrates for novice aquatic gardeners, I would be remiss if I did not at least mention some of the alternative types of substrates that can be used to grow aquatic plants.

The first type of nontraditional substrate includes montmorillonite clay and calcined clay. Montmorillonite clay is the substance used to make many nonclumping cat litter products. Another form of this clay is widely used in products designed to absorb oil spills in garages. The color of most cat litter is not very attractive, but some of the absorbing products are an attractive brown color. If you decide to try one of these products, make sure it is plain, nonclumping, montmorillonite clay with no additives like dyes or perfumes.

Calcined clay is often available as a surface for baseball fields and as a garden pond substrate. It comes in a range of colors from light to dark tan.

The biggest advantage to these products is that they are very inexpensive, so they are an option for those on a tight budget. They also have a very high cation exchange capacity. This feature can be tricky to manage in the first few months of the tank, however, as the clay can capture a large part of the nutrients intended for the plants. If you choose to use these products, be prepared to fertilize heavily in the beginning. Some calcined clays lower the carbonate hardness in the water, which may or may not be advantageous, depending on your local water chemistry. They can also be frustrating to plant in, as they are very lightweight, and plants tend to float out of them until they become well rooted.

Another fairly common alternative substrate for those who prefer a do-it-yourself method is a soil-based one. Some people put a layer of plain garden dirt or organic top-soil under a layer of inert gravel. The gravel holds the soil down so that it makes less of a mess in the water column. The problem is that, as terrestrial gardeners know, not all soils are created equal. Some people report very good results with this method, while others have no end of trouble with algae and with the soil clouding the water.

Another approach is to mineralize the top soil. In this method, soil is screened to remove large pieces of organic material, and then allowed to soak for a time before the water is poured off and the substrate is allowed to dry. The process is repeated a couple of times. Eventually, the more volatile organics have been removed. When placed in the aquarium, the washed soil is capped with inert gravel to keep it out of the water column as much as possible. While this is a much safer and effective approach to a soil substrate, it is time consuming and messy.

There is no doubt that soil substrates provide a much larger amount of the nutrients plants need than many commercial products, and that these nutrients last longer. Unless it is mineralized first, however, the organic material in a soil substrate can make it difficult to handle. I strongly advise those who want to play with alternative substrates to do so in a small tank first. It is less heartbreaking and not as much work if you end up having to tear down a 10-gallon tank because of insurmountable problems as it is to do the same with a 70-gallon tank.

Laterite substrate capped with a clean layer of gravel.

5

FERTILIZERS

ESIDES CARBON DIOXIDE, a number of other nutrients are necessary for good plant growth. Perhaps not surprisingly, we find the same cast of characters that are needed by fully terrestrial plants. In addition, there are a couple of other nutrients that we don't necessarily think about in terrestrial gardening, because they are present in most soils.

For example, both aquatic and terrestrial plants use oxygen and hydrogen, but we normally don't need to worry about these in a planted aquarium since they are in abundant supply in the water itself. Two substances that might not be immediately apparent in an aquarium setting, however, are calcium and magnesium. In many areas of the United States where the water has a reasonable amount of hardness (a general hardness rating of 3 or more), calcium and magnesium will usually be in enough supply to meet the needs of the plants as long as the water is changed regularly. In areas with very soft water, these minerals will need to be added.

MACRONUTRIENTS

Next on the list of nutrients needed is NPK: nitrogen, phosphorus, and potassium. These are major nutrients for aquatic plants just as they are for terrestrial plants. Even so, terrestrial fertilizers are generally not appropriate for aquarium use. One of the big reasons for this is that many terrestrial fertilizers contain nitrogen in the form of urea. In an aquarium, urea quickly becomes toxic ammonia and even more toxic nitrite. It is important that all nitrogen introduced to the aquarium be in the form of nitrate (not to be confused with nitrite). Likewise, phosphorus for aquatic plants needs to be in the form of phosphate.

Macronutrients are available as either commercially prepared liquid planted tank fertilizers or as dry fertilizers from specialty sources. I highly recommend that anyone who is just starting out or only has a small tank purchase supplements from a good, reliable commercial company. As you gain experience or start working with larger tanks, it becomes a more economical option to buy dry chemicals and make your own fertilizers.

The dosing recommendations on commercial fertilizers are very conservative and are meant to keep uninformed people from overdosing their aquariums. I am hoping that by the time you have read this book, you will be well on the way to being an informed aquatic gardener with good lighting and supplemental CO_2. In such a tank, you will find that you need to dose quite a bit more heavily than the minimum doses listed on most commercial products.

For the planted aquarium, nitrate (the preferred form of nitrogen) is usually supplied as potassium nitrate (KNO_3). Phosphate (the preferred form of phosphorus) is usually available as mono-potassium phosphate (KH_2PO_4). Because both of these compounds also contain potassium, it is generally not necessary to dose potassium separately. However, if you feel the need to add a little more potassium, there is little downside. Potassium is available as a ready-made commercial liquid supplement or in dry form as potassium sulfate (K_2SO_4).

It is possible to get test kits to monitor the levels of NPK in your aquarium, and in the beginning, it makes sense to invest in these. Over time, you will get to know how your plants respond to fertilizers, when they need more, and how much. Experienced aquatic gardeners eventually find that they do very little testing, and can judge, just from the look of their plants, what is needed.

Squeeze measure bottles can be very convenient for dosing nutrient solutions, especially if you choose to make your own from dry fertilizers.

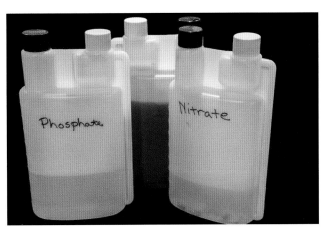

MICRONUTRIENTS

In addition to macronutrients, plants require a number of micronutrients, or trace elements, to grow well. One of these sits in the middle between micro- and macronutrients, and that is iron. It is needed in much lower quantities than the macronutrients, but at much higher levels than the micronutrients boron, copper, chloride, manganese, molybdenum, and zinc.

Again, there are a number of good commercially available liquid trace element fertilizers that include iron, and separate supplements for iron alone. These are a very good place to start. As you become more familiar with fertilizers, especially if you are managing a large tank, you may want to use dry micronutrient compounds as an inexpensive alternative.

Some of these dry compounds have a higher copper level than is needed by aquatic plants. Furthermore, copper is quite toxic to invertebrates, so be aware if you are keeping shrimp in your aquarium. Even with the number and size tanks I run, I choose to use dry fertilizers for my macronutrients and a commercial liquid fertilizer designed for planted aquariums to dose micronutrients.

One more thing that is important to know about iron is that in its pure form it does not remain available to plants in the water column. It must be bound to a chelating agent. Different manufacturers have different ideas about which chelators are best. Some use an inorganic chelator, which binds the iron longer, therefore keeping it in the water column longer. Others feel that an organic chelator is better, specifically because it does break down and the iron becomes available to the plants more quickly. In practice, I have used both types and both work just fine. A supplement with an organic chelator should be dosed in small amounts more often, while one with a good quality inorganic chelator may be dosed in larger amounts less often. The choice is yours.

DOSING NUTRIENTS

Now that you know what nutrients your plants need, you need to decide how much to dose and how often. Unfortunately, there are no quick and easy answers to this. It depends on the kind of substrate you choose, the nutrients (if any) present in your tap

A tank in need of fertilization.

water, the fish and plant load in the tank, how often you change water in the tank, and most importantly, the level of light in your tank.

It is important never to allow the tank to run out of any one nutrient. Some people feel it is important to keep the ratios of macronutrients (NPK) at approximately 10:1:10, but my experience and that of others is that phosphate can be kept somewhat higher than this as long as all nutrients are present in sufficient quantities for growth.

I recommend that you use a nutrient-rich soil-based commercial substrate to give your plants a good start in a new tank. Then slowly start adding liquid supplements after the first month and see how your plants respond.

In the beginning, do water tests for phosphate, nitrate, and iron just after you dose the tank, a few days later, and just before a big water change. This will teach you how your plants are taking up nutrients. If you find that that one of your nutrients is absent several days after dosing, you will know that you need to increase either your dose or the frequency of dosing.

Keep in mind that if your plants have been starved for a while they may take up more nutrients initially and then slow down. If you find increasing levels of nutrients in the water over time, you are feeding your plants more than they can use. This can cause algae problems, but even if it doesn't, it is a waste of fertilizer and a signal to slow down on dosing.

Some people use a system of dosing macros one day and micros the next, for six days of the week, then do a really large water change on the seventh day to bring the levels back down without testing. This method was developed by Tom Barr and is called the Estimative Index, or EI method. The system definitely works, whether you know what is going on in the tank or not, but I believe that someone serious about aquatic gardening, especially if they are in the learning stages, needs to understand what is going on in their tank.

Over time, you will find that you depend less on test kits and more on your eye in evaluating how your plants look to make adjustments to your fertilization routine, just as you do in the garden and with your house plants. That's good. It means that you are learning to manage your tank.

My preferred routine is to dose my tanks twice a week. I find that this works fine to maintain the nutrient levels my plants need and is less work-intensive for me. Over time, you will develop a routine that works well for you.

Same tank after being fertilized regularly for a few weeks.

6

TANK MAINTENANCE

N ADDITION TO THE EQUIPMENT NEEDED to set up your tank, some tools are needed to maintain it. They will make your life much easier in maintaining your tank.

CHANGING WATER

For tanks of 20 gallons or less, you will probably get by very nicely with a siphon hose and a 5-gallon bucket for water changes. Buckets are inexpensive, so buy a new one, write "Aquarium Use Only" on it, and threaten dire consequences to any family member who uses it for washing the car or the kitchen floor. Any chemicals or cleaning products used in the bucket can leach back into water intended for your aquarium, with deadly results. For the health of your plants and animals, you cannot use your aquarium bucket for any other job.

Siphon hoses for aquariums can be purchased at any pet supply source. An aquarium siphon has a wide end, which is used for lightly siphoning mulm from the surface of the substrate and from between plants. You may find directions with your siphon recommending that you drill the tube down into the aquarium substrate to remove dirt. This recommendation is for a fish tank with plain gravel, not for an aquatic garden with specialized substrate and roots growing throughout. Drilling into the substrate of a planted tank damages delicate root systems.

Doing a large water
change with a Python
water change system.

For larger tanks, the tedium of carrying buckets back and forth to the sink may temp you to avoid or reduce the frequency or size of water changes. Not a good idea! So for big tanks, there are specially designed water change systems like the Python that attach directly to the faucet in your kitchen sink and allow you to suck the water out of the tank and replace it directly, never having to lift a bucket. I use one of these systems for all my tanks.

As stated previously, it is far easier to learn to use your local tap water than it is to try to change its chemistry, and this is where that decision really pays off. If you are making substantial changes in your water chemistry, you will need a holding vessel large enough for the water required for your water change. You will need to make all the adjustments there and then find a way to get the water from that container into your tank. If, however, you learn how to use your tap water, you can adjust the water temperature at the tap, put the appropriate amount of chloramine neutralizer directly into your aquarium, and slowly refill the aquarium with tap water. No holding bucket needed.

INSTALLING AND TRIMMING PLANTS

You will also need some tools for planting and trimming your plants. In large tanks, some people start out just using their fingers and a pair of kitchen scissors for these tasks, but as you become more serious about your craft, you will probably want to invest in tools designed specifically for aquascaping. And if you are working in a small tank or planting tiny foreground plants, it is just about impossible to plant by hand. Fortunately, there are tools to help you with this. In particular, you should consider a set of long-handled pinsettes (essentially, very long tweezers) and a pair of long-handled, very sharp trimming scissors.

A good quality pair of pinsettes is vital for doing detailed work in a planted tank. These come in two forms, one with a straight, pointed tip and the other with a curved tip. I prefer the curved pinsettes in most applications, but this is strictly a matter of personal preference. Many excellent aquascapers prefer the straight type.

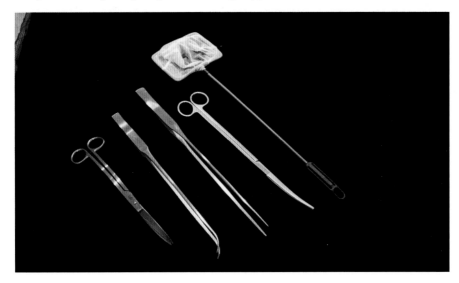

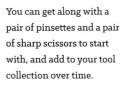

You can get along with a pair of pinsettes and a pair of sharp scissors to start with, and add to your tool collection over time.

Inexpensive tools are available on the internet for as low as $20 or so for a set containing a pair of scissors, one pinsette and, perhaps, a substrate flattening tool. Beware of the false economy of purchasing inexpensive aquascaping tool kits. Most people find that low-cost tools are heavy and unwieldy, and eventually replace them with quality tools. It depends on whether you are willing to buy twice or want to spend the money for good tools from the start. Quality really makes a difference here, so you may want to invest in nicer tools. You will have them for a very long time if you take care of them.

CLEANING GLASS

The aquarium glass will require regular cleaning inside and out. Many tools are specially designed for cleaning aquarium glass, but my favorites come from places other than aquarium shops. For scraping hard algae or lime deposits off glass, I use a razor-edged wallpaper remover. One handle and a supply of extra blades from your local home improvement store will keep you going for years. This is too large a tool for very small tanks, and for these I use a regular safety razor blade.

For soft algae on the inside of the glass, my tool of choice is a melamine foam eraser meant for removing marks from woodwork and other household surfaces. Make sure that you purchase pads that do not contain any additives or cleaning chemicals. The fine abrasive surface of these pads is great for removing algae from the glass and equipment in your tank. Many small nano tanks have rounded corners in the front, which are pretty but can be hard to get into, either with a blade of some sort, or even a large pad. Another useful household item for getting into these tight places is a cotton swab.

Glass covers and even the outside glass on the tank often get a coating of hard-to-remove lime scale on them. Most household cleaners are ammonia based and are not safe for use even near an aquarium. White vinegar to the rescue! Plain white vinegar spread over the glass for a few minutes, then scraped off with a scraper or safety razor will remove all or most of the spots. You can even use it to clean the water line on a rimless tank by drawing the water level down a few inches, applying the vinegar with a paper towel, and then scraping. Avoid getting large quantities of vinegar into the tank, but a few drops will not hurt.

AQUARIUM NETS

You will also need a couple of aquarium nets. It is very hard to catch fish in a heavily planted tank, so fish removal is not usually the purpose of the net if you care for your tank well. But even with the best of care, you may occasionally find a dead fish, and the net will be useful for its removal. More importantly, as you trim your plants, the clippings will pop up to float on the surface. A net can be used to scoop this plant material off, leaving a clean, attractive surface.

Recommended Maintenance Schedule

Regular maintenance results in a healthy aquarium. Some tasks need to be done daily, others are best done weekly or monthly. Here are some suggestions for how often you should service your aquarium and what things need attention.

Daily maintenance

- Feed fish and shrimp
- Check CO_2 flow
- Check drop checker
- Check pressure in CO_2 cylinder (if it drops below 800 PSI, replace or refill)
- Observe the fish for health and normal behavior
- Observe plants for signs of algae or nutrient deficiencies

Every 2–4 days

- Fertilize plants, adjusting the amount and frequency to suit your tank. Remember that commercial fertilizer recommendations are on the low side to keep people from causing problems in their tanks. You may have to dose considerably more than the starter doses listed on the label.

Weekly

- Change 50 percent of water (adjust to suit your tank's needs, but no less that 25 percent weekly and more is usually better)
- Make sure that filter intake is clear
- Clean glass, inside and out
- Trim plants as needed

Monthly

- Change filter media

WHILE YOU'RE AWAY

The nice thing about aquatic gardens is that they don't need the frequent watering that most houseplants do. As long as your maintenance routine has been good and the tank is in good condition, it is perfectly fine to leave a planted tank for a week to 10 days with no care at all and no changes in routine. The fish will pick at the biofilm in the tank, and while they will be pleased to see the supplier-of-food when you get back, they will be none the worse for their period of fasting. Plants are able to store luxury-use amounts of nutrients, so as long as they are well fed prior to your departure, they can easily live off this during your time away. When you come home, you can resume your regular maintenance routine.

A longer period away, up to one month or so, needs to be handled a little differently. If you have a low to moderately lit tank with slow-growth plants, you can probably get by having someone come in twice a week to feed your fish. This will also provide some nutrients for your plants and will tide them over until your return. We have handled classroom tanks very successfully this way, even over summer break.

Be very careful that the person who feeds your fish knows how to do this without overfeeding. If you have the slightest question about the person's ability to handle this job, make it simple for them and safe for your tank. I use small pill boxes and put just one feeding in each compartment, a separate box for each tank. This way there can be no costly mistakes. If the tank is small or uncovered, you may also need your aquarium-sitter to top up the tanks for evaporation as needed.

If you have a fast-growth, high light, CO_2-driven system, you will need a little more preparation for a long absence. First, make sure your CO_2 tank is full, so there is no chance of it running out while you are gone. Leave the CO_2 running at its normal level while you are away. Trim the fast-growing stem plants back hard, so that it will take them some time to reach the surface of the water again. Reduce the light intensity in the tank to approximately half of what you normally run. If that is not possible, reduce the photoperiod to between six and eight hours per day.

Then have your helper come in twice weekly to feed the fish and top up water as mentioned above, but also have them fertilize the plants. Have them use approximately half the dose you normally use, and mark the fertilizer bottles clearly. If you have more than one tank, you may want to tape specific directions to the front of each tank. As soon as is reasonably possible after you get home, do a very large (70- to 90-percent) water change on your tanks, remove any algae, and trim the plants as needed.

Handling even high light, fast-growth systems in this way, I have never come home to a major problem in a tank, in spite of being away for three weeks or more at a time at least twice a year. The most common cause of serious trouble in planted aquariums over vacations is either overfeeding the fish or loss of CO_2, so make sure you plan proactively to prevent those problems and your tank will be fine when you get home.

7

Good local independent stores often carry a nice selection of healthy plants.

UST AS WITH GARDEN PLANTS, aquarium plants come in so many species and varieties that there is no way I can address them all. Even if I tried, more are discovered or developed every year. There are already very good resources for identifying and learning about specific plants, and you can find those in the resource section at the end of this book. But I will start you off with some hardy, easy-to-grow species that are also readily available. Once you get your "hands wet," you can branch out and experiment with less common, more difficult or more expensive plants.

Beware of purchasing plants at the big box pet stores. Some of these plants are fine, but others are terrestrial plants being sold as aquarium plants. They are not, and they *will* die if kept under water. If you purchase plants at these places, do your homework first and know what you are buying. Depending on where you live, you may find that your local independent fish store has a good selection of truly aquatic plants. If not, many can special order plants that you want.

For more unusual plants, however, many people find that trading with others in local aquarium societies on the internet is the way to go. As you get more involved, you will start to network with more people and new possibilities will unfold.

As with garden plants, aquarium plants can be roughly divided into those that need higher or lower levels of light. Those that need higher amounts of light generally also need supplemental CO_2 in the aquarium. Some plants do well only in very soft or very hard water, but the majority of plants can be grown under a wide range of water conditions as long as their basic needs for light, CO_2, and nutrients are adequately met.

LOW LIGHT OPTIONS

Among the easiest aquarium plants are those that thrive even under low light conditions. While these plants will benefit from supplemental CO_2, it is definitely not a requirement. Plants that require little light are frequently considered the old standbys of the aquarium world and are often the first introduction many fish tank keepers have to aquatic plants.

Plants in this group will usually get by even on the meager light supplied with beginner kit aquariums. If the tank is appropriately stocked with fish, low light plants may do fine without the need for any feeding beyond what is introduced to the tank through fish food and fish waste. That doesn't mean that they will do well and look good without care, however. You will still need to do regular water changes to avoid algae problems.

Anubias barteri var. *coffeefolia* is a particularly beautiful variant.

Anubias barteri

Common name: none
Origin: Southeast Nigeria, Equatorial Guinea, and Cameroon
Growth rate: Slow to moderate

Several *Anubias* species are available for aquariums, but the most common, by far, are subspecies and cultivars of *Anubias barteri*. This species is one of the toughest of all aquarium plants and will put up with abuse that almost nothing else will. It has tough leaves that even withstand many fish that will decimate most other plants.

In nature, *Anubias barteri* grows with its roots over and around rocks in areas where it is sometimes submersed and other times emersed. The rhizome should not be buried in the substrate or it will rot. Instead, tie the plant to a stone or piece of drift wood using either cotton thread or garden ties and place these where you want the plants to grow. Before long, the plants will grow roots down off this structure and into the substrate.

All *Anubias* plants are easily divided by cutting the rhizome with a sharp knife or scissors. One of the most delightful aspects of *Anubias* is that it is of the few plant groups that will flower under water. The flowers look similar to a tiny peace lily, not surprisingly, since both are members of the family *Araceae*.

The most common form for aquariums is *Anubias barteri* var. *barteri*. While it is a slow-growing plant, especially in less-than-optimum conditions, over time it can reach at least 18 inches tall and fill an aquarium from end to end.

Next down in size is *Anubias barteri* var. *coffeefolia*. It has shorter petioles and attractive, deeply veined leaves. It grows even slower than var. *barteri*, making it a wonderful midground plant in a good-sized aquarium.

Smaller still is *Anubias barteri* var. *nana*. Leaves of this variety range from ovate to cordate and the petioles are relatively short. Because the entire plant is smaller than the other varieties, it is a great candidate for smaller tanks, but also makes a nice contrast to the large-leaved *Anubias* in a larger tank.

The smallest member of this group is *Anubias barteri* var. *nana* 'Petite'. It is a cultivar (manmade variety), originally developed by Oriental Aquarium in Singapore. It tends to be a bit more expensive than other types of *Anubias*, but is well worth the price, as it is hardy and easy to grow. It is indispensable in nano tanks, especially for those who want a low light, slow-growth tank. If it has a downside, it is that it can be a bit harder to get the tiny roots and rhizomes tied to rocks or branches. It is well worth the effort, however.

Here, *Anubias barteri* var. *nana* 'Petite' has been tucked in among rugged rock work to good effect.

Anubias barteri has large, leathery leaves and is tough enough to
stand up to all but the most determined plant-eating fish. ▲

Bucephalandra species

Common name: variable
Origin: Borneo
Growth rate: Slow

Bucephalandra is relatively new on the aquarium scene. Plants are currently high priced and rarely found in local aquarium stores, but they are becoming more common, and the price is going down. They are definitely worth mentioning because many are well suited to small, low to moderately lit tanks. They are now being produced through tissue culture, so we will see even more available over time.

Bucephalandra is an aroid, like *Anubias* and *Cryptocoryne*, and like those two genera, it includes species that are more suited to aquatic life than others. Stick to the less expensive, more common types until you learn more about them, as these are also the ones most likely to do well in aquariums. Like *Anubias*, *Bucephalandra* species usually do best tied to a small stone or wood, where their rhizome can stay above the substrate. Over time, the roots will find their way down and into the substrate. Their growth is quite slow and most plants stay small, but they have the delightful habit of flowering under water, something you see only in a few aquatic plants.

Bucephalandra species are highly sought after little plants for good reason. The best are pretty and easy to grow.

Ceratophyllum demersum

The fluffy plant on the left is *Ceratophyllum demersum*.

Common name: Hornwort
Origin: Widespread, either naturally or by introduction
Growth rate: Fast

Ceratophyllum was one of the earliest plants in aquarium use, simply because it is so easy to keep. It doesn't care if it is planted in the substrate (where it will develop rhizoids to hold itself in place) or left floating, though it grows faster and branches more once it has hit the surface. It is an obligate aquatic species and never grows above the surface of the water. Because it is very fast-growing, *Ceratophyllum* is not a good candidate for the small aquarium, but in a large tank can be a wonderful nutrient sponge in a tank that is heavily stocked with fish.

Ceratophyllum demersum in the wild in Kerala, India. This plant can be found in tropical and temperate areas worldwide

Cryptocoryne species

Cryptocoryne species come in a wide variety of leaf shapes and colors. Commercially propagated plants are mostly hardy, beautiful, and tolerant of a wide range of conditions.

Common name: none
Origin: Southeast Asia and India
Growth rate: Slow to moderate

Cryptocoryne is a large genus and many of its species are suitable aquarium plants. Most do well in lower light aquariums. They range in size from the tiny *C. parva*, which makes a great foreground plant in a low light tank, to huge plants with straplike leaves, like *C. aponogetifolia*.

The most commonly available commercially produced *Cryptocoryne* is *C. wendtii* and its many forms, including several color variations. These are extremely hardy and attractive plants ranging from solid green to reddish brown. In tanks with more light, they tend to stay lower and are bushier, while in lower light tanks, they are likely to get taller with longer petioles (leaf stems). Either way they are lovely.

Hydrocotyle leucocephala

Common name: Pennywort
Origin: Mexico in the north through Argentina in the south
Growth rate: Moderate to fast

There are a number of species of *Hydrocotyle*, but only a few are good aquarium plants. The largest and easiest of these is *H. leucocephala*. It can be planted in the substrate, then will slowly chain its way upward toward the surface. It can be trimmed between nodes and replanted elsewhere in the aquarium.

Hydrocotyle leucocephala has a vinelike growth habit and can be allowed to grow vertically or be trained to creep horizontally.

Hygrophila corymbosa

Common name: Giant hygro, temple plant
Origin: Southeast Asia
Growth rate: Moderate to fast

Giant hygro is a fast-growing stem plant available in several different leaf shapes, though they are all members of the same species. It is a great plant for the larger tank with low to moderate light levels. While this is another plant that will grow much better with supplemental CO_2, it is also quite capable of doing well even in tanks without supplementation. Because of its large size, it is best planted in the substrate toward the back of the aquarium. When *Hygrophila* is allowed to grow up out of the water, it often treats the aquarist to the sight of small but attractive purple flowers.

Hygrophila corymbosa, the plant at the back of this photo with lance-shaped foliage, is hardy, attractive, and a fast grower.

Lomariopsis cf. *lineata*

Common name: Süsswassertang
Origin: Unknown
Growth rate: Slow but steady if not disturbed

This unusual little plant is actually the gametophyte form of a terrestrial fern. No one is sure why it can maintain this aquatic form indefinitely, but it can and does. It is not as fast growing as some of the aquatic mosses and is lovey tucked in places where water flow is minimal. The plant is able to grow into a mound or ball shape. It is very undemanding and does well even in the lowest light tanks. Unfortunately, you will often see this plant sold, incorrectly, as "Subwassertang" by people who don't understand that the letter "ß" in the original German name is properly translated as "ss," not as the Latin letter "b."

Lomariopsis cf. *lineata* is more commonly known as Süsswassertang, which literally means "freshwater seaweed."

Marsilea hirsuta

Common name: Miniature four-leaf clover
Origin: Australia
Growth rate: Slow to moderate

Marsilea hirsuta is actually a small fern that grows hugging the ground, emersed in marshy areas or completely submersed. When grown emersed, it lives up to its four-leaf clover name. Submersed, it tends to have only one leaflet per petiole.

There are several *Marsilea* species that do well in aquariums, but the others are all quite a bit taller, and some will grow right to the surface. The advantage of *M. hirsuta* is that it is one of a very few plants that can be used as a ground cover in a relatively low light tank. The growth will be slower in low light, but it will continue to spread slowly.

Marsilea hirsuta is one of the best options for a foreground plant in a low to moderate light tank.

This is a needle-leaf form of the highly variable *Microsorum pteropus*.

Microsorum pteropus

Common name: Java fern
Origin: Tropical Asia
Growth rate: Slow to moderate

Java fern is an amphibious fern that, in the wild, often grows in the spray zone of waterfalls. In the wild, it is a plant that most often inhabits shady areas in nature, so will grow nicely under low light in the aquarium. It grows slowly, but will continue to produce new leaves even under these conditions, eventually producing nice thick stands of dark green leaves. There are a number of varieties, ranging from the "normal" long, broad-leaved types, to fine, narrow-leaved varieties and the much smaller varieties, 'Windeløv', which has fine, lacy ends on the leaves and 'Trident', with its long, fingerlike leaf edges.

Microsorum pteropus is a very variable species. Here a small variant of the species was used to completely cover the back and sides of a tank. ▲

Microsorum pteropus 'Trident' has long, fingerlike leaf edges. ▲

A large-leaved form of *Microsorum pteropus* is anchored on either side by red-foliaged plants, a *Ludwigia* species on the left and *Rotala macrandra* on the right. ◄

Taxiphyllum barbieri

Common name: Java moss
Origin: Asia
Growth rate: Fast

Java moss is the most common of a number of aquatic mosses now available for aquarium use. It will grow easily and quickly even in low light, and is very popular with those who breed aquarium fish, as it gives baby fish a wonderful place to hide and feed. In the aquatic garden, it can be attached to stones or wood for lovely accents. It will also grow if just allowed to float free, but tends to get wound around other plants unless you trim it back regularly.

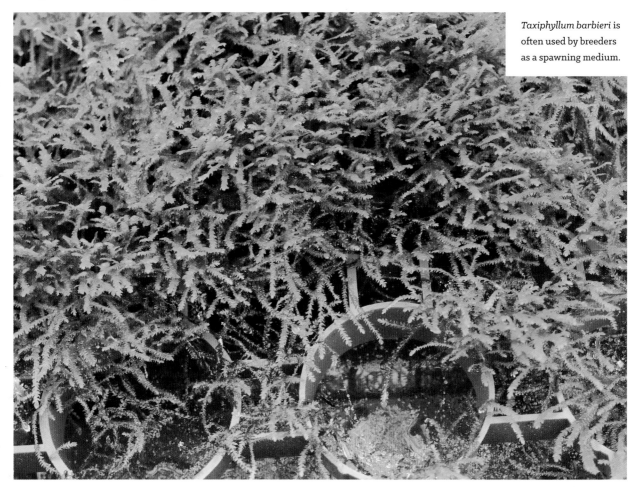

Taxiphyllum barbieri is often used by breeders as a spawning medium.

MODERATE LIGHT OPTIONS

Aponogeton crispus is often available as a dry bulb in chain pet stores. It can be fun to take this dry bulb home and see it magically sprout in the aquarium.

Moderate light plants generally require more light than would come with the typical kit fish tank, but do not require very strong light to grow. In fact, a few can limp along in a way many people find satisfactory even in lower light levels. Such plants will, however, be more robust and show better color in a tank with higher light. Most will also be at their best only with supplemental CO_2 and regular nutrient supplementation.

Aponogeton species

Common name: varies with species
Origin: Tropical and subtropical Old World
Growth rate: Fast

The commonly available *Aponogeton* species in the trade are lovely plants and quite easy to grow. They can even be found as dry bulbs in the pet department of big box stores. Usually either *A. crispus* or a hybrid variety are available in these stores. The bulbs grow easily when just placed in the substrate. Like terrestrial bulbs, aquatic bulbs contain the initial nutrients needed by the plants, giving them a great head start. However, just like all other plants, without proper nutrient supplementation, their lives will be limited.

Some *Aponogeton* species have a dormant period when they die back. However this is not usually a problem with the more commonly available species and hybrids. Most *Aponogeton* species are relatively large plants, so should be placed toward the back of the aquarium.

There are some very special species of *Aponogeton* that come from the island of Madagascar, the most well known of these being *A. madagascariensis*, or the Madagascar lace plant. This striking plant has a lacy appearance formed by the lack of tissue between the veins in the plant leaves. Madagascar lace plant requires a little more care than the more common types of *Aponogeton*, so practice first with the easier species. The other thing to keep in mind with this species is that when it does do well, it becomes a monster-sized plant, suitable only to the largest of home aquariums (90 gallons or larger).

Aponogeton cf. crispus in a pond in India.

Lack of tissue between
the veins gives leaves of
Aponogeton madagascariensis
a lacy appearance. ▲

Aponogetons are another one of those magical plants that are likely to bloom in the aquarium to the delight of newer aquatic gardeners. Better yet, many species are self-fertile and will set seed. If you collect these seeds and place them in shallow water on a soil-based substrate, your little aponogetons will sprout and develop into plants that you can use in other places or trade with friends.

Bolbitis heudelotii

Common name: none
Origin: Africa
Growth rate: Moderate

Bolbitis heudelotii is a lovely fern that can get very large under good growth conditions, but it can also be kept smaller by frequent trimming and by using smaller sections of rhizome. The plant does not tolerate being planted in the substrate well. It does best tied to a piece of wood, though it can also be tied to stones.

Bolbitis heudelotii contributes deep green transparent-looking fronds with good texture.

Cabomba caroliniana is best planted in groups toward the back of the aquarium.

Cabomba caroliniana

Common name: none
Origin: Eastern United States
Growth rate: Very fast

This frilly stem plant is an obligate aquatic plant which never grows on land. It is familiar to most people who have spent time swimming in eastern lakes and ponds, since it is common in the shallow areas of most of them. *Cabomba caroliniana* is an easy-to-grow plant that will require regular trimming or it can take over. There are a number of other *Cabomba* species available too, but none are as easy to grow as this one. Be aware that this plant has the potential to be invasive, as is seen in increasingly northern states in the United States. Please dispose of clippings responsibly.

A broad-leaved form of *Ceratopteris thalictroides*.

Ceratopteris thalictroides is seen here growing in a river in southern India. It is widespread throughout Southeast Asia.

Ceratopteris thalictroides

Common name: Water sprite
Origin: Southeast Asia, India, northern Australia
Growth rate: Very fast

This aquatic fern is an old-time favorite among aquarists. It is one of the very easiest plants to grow, doing well under a wide variety of conditions. It can be rooted in the substrate or left floating on the surface, where the roots will trail in the water. It is a wonderful plant for taking up excess nutrients in a predominantly fish tank, and also provides good cover for baby fish.

As the plant grows, it will develop young plants that can be removed and planted elsewhere in the tank. Even a single leaf left floating on the water surface will develop into a new plant. If water sprite has a fault, it is that it is such a strong grower that it can crowd out other plants or become a nuisance to maintain. But this plant, probably more than any other single species, has given many aquarists their first taste of aquatic gardening.

A fine-leaved form of
Ceratopteris thalictroides.

Didiplis diandra

Common name: none
Origin: Eastern United States
Growth rate: Fast

Didiplis diandra is a very pretty, small-leaved plant that is an excellent candidate for the smaller planted aquarium. Although it can also be grown in large masses in bigger tanks, the tiny leaves make it a very useful addition to the smaller tank.

It was once thought that *Didiplis* needed strong light to survive in the aquarium, but experienced aquarists have found that the plant does quite well with moderate light, as long as there is an adequate supply of supplemental CO_2. Under good conditions the plant produces very pretty bronze tips that are worth any extra effort it requires. Under conditions not to its liking, which includes aquariums where water is not changed frequently enough, it is common for the stems to become brittle and start to rot.

Didiplis diandra has unique, airy foliage not easily replicated in other aquarium plants. Under strong light, the tips bring a lovely bronze highlight to the tank.

Echinodorus species

Common name: Sword plant
Origin: New World, from southern North America south throughout South America
Growth rate: Moderate

Leaves of *Echinodorus* 'Ozelot' are beautiful with lovely red spotting. Just be aware that these plants get large.

Echinodorus is the *Hemerocallis* of the aquarium world: like daylilies, sword plants are the source every year of numerous cultivars that are developed and released to the public. These new plants tend to be quite expensive, and then the price goes down over time, as they become more commonly available. The plants range from moderately sized to some that are best housed only in very large tanks. They vary both in leaf shape and color, with variations of reds, greens, spots, and changeable leaves predominating. There are also a large number of wild species, but, as with daylilies, these are harder to find commercially. For the new aquatic gardener, the readily available cultivars give plenty of room for discovery and experimentation.

Sword plants form rosettes, where the leaves and roots grow from a single crown. Most types will produce flower stalks that rise up out of the aquarium if they have the chance. Once they are above the water, clusters of small white flowers form, followed by small plantlets at the site of each cluster. As these plantlets grow and develop roots, they can be cut off the mother plant and used in other places.

The larger species and cultivars are robust plants and heavy feeders. If they are not fed regularly, either through supplementation of the water column or root feeding, they can either stunt or start to outcompete other plants in the aquarium. They also develop a very large root system that can disrupt a large section of the aquarium if you decide to uproot them. If you must move one, use a sharp knife to cut down through the substrate, straight toward the bottom of the tank, in a ring around the plant. Then when you pull the plant up, you will disturb as small a part of the aquarium as possible. The roots that are left behind in the substrate will deteriorate and provide food for the other plants in your tank.

Eleocharis species

Common name: Hairgrass
Origin: Worldwide
Growth rate: Moderate

Eleocharis species are lovely grasslike plants. A number of species are available commercially, ranging from very short *Eleocharis* sp. "Belém" to long types better suited to the back or the aquarium. One species, *E. vivipara*, produces plantlets on the tips of the leaves. Some people really like the way this looks, while others find it a bit messy looking. The choice is yours.

Eleocharis parvulus makes a very nice ground cover in the left front of this tank.

Helanthium species

Common name: Chain sword
Origin: New World, from southern North America south throughout South America
Growth rate: Moderate

For many years, species in this genus were considered part of the genus *Echinodorus*. Within the last few years, they have been moved to their own genus, based on a number of differences including the fact that *Helanthium* species reproduce via runner through the substrate while *Echinodorus* species do not, and the fact that although most *Echinodorus* species hybridize easily, *Helanthium* species do not hybridize with *Echinodorus*, even under laboratory conditions. In practice,

however, you will find *Helanthium* sp. sold as chain swords, and sometimes still labeled erroneously as "*Echinodorus*."

One way or the other, chain swords are very useful in moderately lit tanks. They spread along the foreground of the tank, but stay low, so they don't hide the plants behind them. Two species are commonly available, *Helanthium tenellum*, narrow-leaved chain sword, and *H. bolivianum*, broad-leaved chain sword. The latter is a little taller than the former and has broader leaves.

In recent years a little cultivar with curly leaves, named *Helanthium bolivianum* 'Vesuvius' has become available on the market. It is an attractive little curiosity and grows just the way the species does.

Helanthium bolivianum is the small, grassy plant in the left foreground.

Hydrocotyle tripartita

Common name: none
Origin: Southeast Asia
Growth rate: Fast

Hydrocotyle tripartita is a much smaller, lacier, and slightly less rampant grower than *H. leucocephala*. It does best with some supplemental CO_2, but will still grow slowly in a tank without. It can be used in just one area of the tank or can be used as a lovely, fast-growing foreground plant, though if it is used this way, it will require frequent trimming.

Hydrocotyle tripartita forms a dense carpet.

Hygrophila difformis

Common name: Water wisteria
Origin: India east to the Malaysian peninsula
Growth rate: Fast

Hygrophila difformis is a lovely plant that is often confused with *Ceratopteris thalictroides*, water sprite. Although both plants have pinnate foliage when grown submersed, *H. difformis* is a flowering stem plant, while *C. thalictroides* is a fern, with stems growing from a single crown. In its emersed state, *H. difformis* has lanceolate to elliptical leaves. This sometimes takes aquarists by surprise if the plants purchased have been grown in the emersed state before being placed in the aquarium.

Hygrophila difformis is an easy-to-grow aquarium plant that places minimal demands on the aquarist. Moderate light and CO_2 will have it growing extremely well. It does tend to get pale if it doesn't receive enough nutrients, but even this will only slow its growth unless neglect goes on for a very long time.

Hygrophila difformis is a traditional aquarium plant.

Ludwigia species

Common name: none
Origin: Temperate and tropical areas around the world
Growth rate: Fast

Ludwigia species are varied, and some are much more difficult than others to propagate in the aquarium. The types that most often change hands between aquarists are usually among those species native to North, Central, and South America. *Ludwigia* species also hybridize quite easily—sometimes even in the wild—so there are many intermediate forms as well.

The easiest and most common species for an aquarium are *Ludwigia repens*, *L. palustris*, and a cross between the two. These species and their hybrid offspring are easy to grow and bring some nice red color to the moderately lit aquarium. They will grow even in tanks without supplemental CO_2, but, as with most plants, prosper when it is provided.

Ludwigia species tend to branch strongly as they approach the water surface. This can be pretty, but you must also watch that they do not block the light to plants below.

Ludwigia repens can bring a nice pop of color to even a moderately lit tank with the bright red undersides of its leaves. These plants have not yet changed over to their submersed form, which typically is even redder.

Nymphaea lotus "Red," also sold as *N. zenkeri* "Red," comes from West Africa. While it can produce flowers, it is kept by most people because of its beautiful foliage.

Nymphaea species and hybrids

Common name: none
Origin: Temperate to tropical areas worldwide
Growth rate: Moderate

The genus *Nymphaea* encompasses all the plants known in the pond gardening world as water lilies. Everyone is familiar with their floating lily pads and lovely flowers in the wild as well as in garden ponds. What is less well known outside the aquarium world is that some species and hybrids stay quite small and make lovely aquarium plants. Although the types used in aquariums are perfectly capable of producing floating leaves, and even flowers, they are kept because they produce many, often beautifully colored submersed leaves. Often, a hybrid variety such as *N. zenkeri* "Red" is one of the first really red plants that an aquarist is successful with.

These species and hybrids are among the easiest of plants, requiring just good normal care. The one trick to them is that they will, from time to time, shoot a floating leaf to the surface. If you nip these in the bud, before the leaf can reach the surface, the plant will continue to produce the low, underwater leaves. Once one leaf makes it to the surface, the plant is likely to bolt, sending up more and more floating leaves. This can be a problem because the leaves will shade light from all your plants below. However, it's not the end of the world. Cut off all the leaves right above the bulb. If well nourished, the plant will start to produce more underwater leaves.

Occasionally, a person with a very large tank will decide to allow their *Nymphaea* plant to continue to produce floating leaves in one end of the tank. Those that choose this option are often treated to a lovely night-blooming water flower on the top of their tank.

Under good conditions, *Rotala rotundifolia* turns a bright rosy hue on top.

Rotala rotundifolia

Common name: none
Origin: Southeast Asia
Growth rate: Fast

Rotala rotundifolia is an easy-to-grow stem plant. It is useful in small tanks because of its small leaf size and in large tanks because it can be trimmed into large, dense bushes. It will grow slowly even under fairly low light and without supplemental CO_2, but you won't see the true beauty of this plant without stronger light and CO_2. Under good conditions some varieties, including those most commonly available commercially, turn a bright rosy hue on top. There are a number of varieties some with fanciful names, ranging from solid green to deep magenta in color. The redder they are, the more they will need optimal aquarium conditions to look their best.

Rotala rotundifolia in the wild showing both submersed and emersed growth. ▲

127

Vallisneria species

Common name: none
Origin: Temperate and tropical regions worldwide
Growth rate: Fast

Vallisneria is an undemanding plant with long, tapelike leaves. The foliage varies from narrow-leaved types with leaves less than a tenth inch to broad-leaved types with leaves almost 1 inch wide. Plants with the latter leaves should be reserved for only the largest tanks, because the leaves are also capable of growing over 7 feet long.

Vallisneria species spread through the substrate by runner and are capable of taking over quite a bit of territory. Some people like that effect, but you should consider it before deciding to use this species in your aquarium. In any case, *Vallisneria* should be planted at the back and sides of the tank, with shorter plants in front.

Vallisneria growing in the back left of this beautiful, moderately lit tank. ▼

Vallisneria in a stream in India. ▼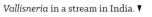

This selection barely touches the many aquarium plants that can be grown under higher light, with a steady supply of supplemental CO_2 and regular nutrient supplementation. As you become more adept at managing your tank, you can spread out and try many other species as well, but here I have tried to give you an idea of just a few of the beautiful, varied plants that can be kept in a well-managed planted aquarium. Remember that you can always choose plants from a lower light category to add to the variety in your well-lit, CO_2-supplemented tank, but you can't always go in the other direction.

In good light, foliage of *Blyxa aubertii* turns bronze-red.

Alternanthera reineckii is a blazing red plant from its leaves right down to its stem.

Alternanthera reineckii

Common name: none
Origin: South America
Growth rate: Moderate

This species makes a real statement in the aquarium and is one of the easiest red plants to grow. Several cultivars are available; all are slightly different shades of red, pink, and violet. With its largish leaves, *Alternanthera reineckii* looks best in very large tanks and when used for just a pop of color here or there. It can be easy to get carried away with red.

There is also a smaller variety, *Alternanthera reineckii* 'Mini', which has smaller leaves and also stays shorter. Though this plant will also require regular trimming, it does not grow anywhere near as fast as the species.

Blyxa japonica

Common name: none
Origin: From India east to Japan, south to New Guinea, not found in Australia
Growth rate: Moderate

Blyxa japonica is a lovely plant that forms tufts of bright green leaves with a silvery sheen. Each plant produces many offshoots that can be removed and planted in new places in the aquarium. This species makes a beautiful midground accent or can even be used at the back of very small tanks.

Another species, *Blyxa aubertii*, is also lovely, but quite a bit taller. This species has a tendency to become a bronze-red color under strong lighting. Because of its larger size, *B. aubertii* is a better candidate for the back of the aquarium.

Blyxa japonica makes a beautiful grasslike midground accent.

Hemianthus glomeratus has a pleasing mound-shape habit.

Hemianthus glomeratus

Common name: Pearl grass, baby's tears
Origin: Southeastern United States
Growth rate: Moderate

Hemianthus glomeratus is a lovely plant with a very confusing naming history. First are the two common names, both of which are also used for other plants both aquatic and terrestrial (which it is why it's better to stick with scientific names). But even its scientific name has been somewhat a mess. Originally, this plant changed hands under the name *Micranthemum micranthemoides*. Then the genus name was changed from *Micranthemum* to *Hemianthus*. Next, thanks to the detective work of Cavan Allen, it turned out that the real *Hemianthus micranthemoides* has not been seen alive since 1941 and may, in fact, be extinct. The plant that we have been enjoying in our tanks is actually *H. glomeratus*.

Now that we have the tricky name business out of the way, *Hemianthus glomeratus* is a lovely, small-leaved plant that grows in a pleasing mound shape with just a little trimming. It is a perfect candidate for nano tanks, but is also quite useful in the foreground areas of larger tanks.

Ludwigia arcuata

Common name: none
Origin: Southeastern United States
Growth rate: Fast

Ludwigia arcuata is the best of the *Ludwigia* species
for small tanks. It has small, thin, needle-shaped
leaves with a lovely rosy color in good light. It does
not grow quite as fast as *L. repens* and some of the
more common *Ludwigia* crosses, so between that
and the smaller leaf size and more graceful habit, it
is a better choice for a small tank. That said, it can be
extremely beautiful massed in a larger tank. The plant
branches and gets very bushy if trimmed regularly.

Ludwigia arcuata adds color to any aquarium.

Myriophyllum mattogrossense

Common name: none
Origin: Ecuador, Brazil, and Peru
Growth rate: Very fast

Myriophyllum mattogrossense is a lovely, very fast growing stem plant. For the novice aquatic gardener, it is hard to think of a more satisfying plant. When given good light, supplemental CO_2, and regular feeding, it produces huge amounts of beautiful, bright green fluffy growth. When it gets too large, simply divide it, replant what you'd like to keep, and give the rest away to friends. Many species of *Myriophyllum* are available, but *M. mattogrossense* is both beautiful and easy to grow, making it a most commendable beginner's plant.

Myriophyllum mattogrossense (center front) has light green feathery foliage.

Pogostemon helferi is highly prized for its crinkly, starlike foliage.

Pogostemon helferi growing emersed and flowering in its type locality in Thailand. ▲

Pogostemon helferi

Common name: Downoi (Thai for "Little Star")
Origin: Western Thailand and Myanmar
Growth rate: Moderate

This lovely little carpet plant is relatively new on the aquarium plant scene, having been discovered in the early 2000s. It requires strong light and supplemental CO_2, and does not do well in very soft water, but as long as its needs are met, it is a good grower. It is unique in looks, with its crinkled leaves and mounded growth habit.

Pogostemon helferi is available in pots, but these tend to be quite expensive for only very few plants. Recently, it has become available in tissue culture packs. You get six or more small plants for a very reasonable price. When these are given good growing conditions, they fill out quickly and you will have more plants than you need.

Rotala macrandra

Common name: none
Origin: Southern India
Growth rate: Fast

Rotala macrandra in its submersed form is a very fragile plant and must be handled carefully to avoid crushing the leaves or stems, but when it is happy with its growing conditions, you could hardly find a prettier plant. It is a bright, rosy pink, with lovely, wavy-edged leaves. Once it is established in the tank, it is a very fast, strong grower.

The leaves of Rotala macrandra bring a beautiful splash of color to the planted aquarium. The plants photosynthesize heavily, so the leaves often sparkle with oxygen bubbles.

Rotala macrandra flowers are bright, rosy pink.

Staurogyne "Porto Velho" is the working name for this plant which has not been scientifically named at this point. ◄

Staurogyne repens

Common name: none
Origin: Mato Grosso region of Brazil
Growth rate: Moderate

Staurogyne repens is another attractive carpet plant for higher light tanks. Some people are able to grow it in more moderate light and without supplemental CO_2, but that is not the rule. It will definitely grow faster, cleaner, and make a nicer carpet with better light and CO_2 levels.

Several other *Staurogyne* species are available now, most of which are low growing, like *S. repens*. One, however, *S. bihar*, is a very large but attractive stem plant that should be planted at the back of a good-sized aquarium.

Staurogyne repens makes a great carpet plant.

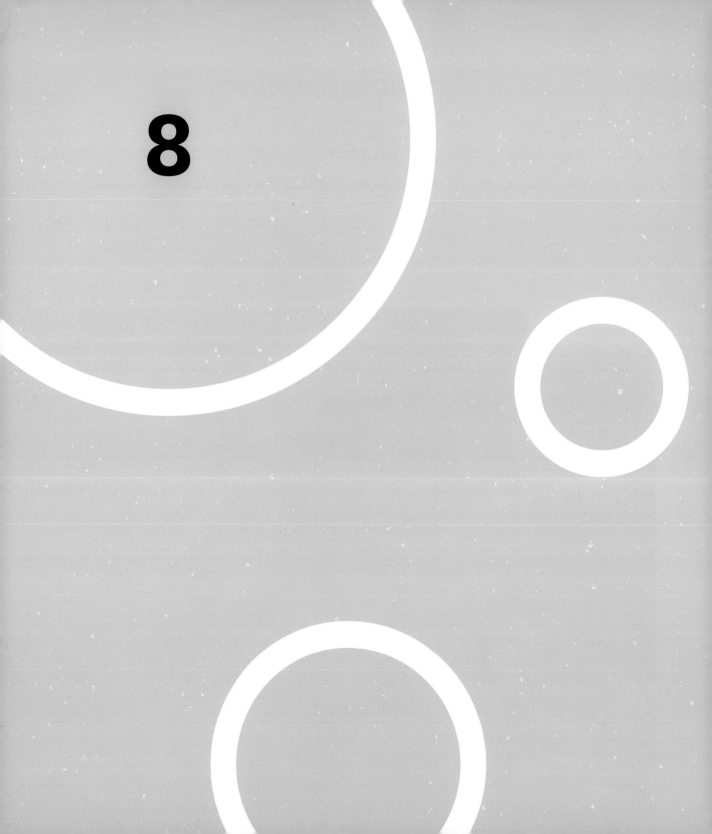

8

PLANT CARE

It is important that crown plants be buried in substrate only to the crown. All the leaves must be above the substrate or they will rot.

 NCE YOU HAVE DECIDED ON WHICH PLANTS to include in your aquarium, you'll need to install them in the tank. Eventually they will grow and need to be trimmed or divided. You may even want to learn how to propagate new plants. In this chapter we will consider various plant types and how to care for them.

PLANTING TECHNIQUES

It is not surprising that given the different types of plants available, they require different methods of planting in your tank. Some plants do best in the substrate, while others do best attached to wood or stone. Some plants are large enough that they can be put in place with your hands, while other, tiny plants need to be planted with special tools.

Crown Plants

Crown plants are those where the leaves grow up from a central crown, while the roots grow down from that same crown. Most of these are good-sized plants, like the many *Echinodorus* species and hybrids and *Ceratopteris thalictroides*.

Although you may also find it bare-rooted, this type of plant is most often sold in a small plastic pot, with the roots embedded in rock wool. The roots may still be completely within the pot, in which case, you can just slide the entire mass of rock wool out of the pot. If the roots have started to grow out through the pot, you will need to cut the pot apart with sharp scissors so that you can get the pot off without damaging the roots.

The next step is to remove as much of the rock wool as possible. Try to peel it off with your fingers, but if the plant has been in its pot for a long time, you may have to resort to using tweezers under running water to get the majority of the rock wool out. You don't need to get every single bit out, but the rock wool doesn't break down, and can be a nuisance floating around in the tank. It is important to remove the majority of the rock wool, because it has been soaked in nutrients while the plant was growing in the greenhouse. Large, unexpected nutrient additions can cause algae problems in your tank. Removing the rock wool avoids this potential problem.

Finally, trim the roots to a reasonable length. Unless the plant is extremely large, roots longer than 3–4 inches are unnecessary. Just as with a garden plant, if the plant has become pot bound, so that the roots are running in a circle around the pot, make some vertical slices into the root mass. This will encourage the plant to start sending out roots in new directions.

Crown plants are quite easy to plant by hand. Use your fingers to guide the roots down into the substrate. Go a little deeper than you want the plant to sit when you are finished, and then lightly pull up on the plant to expose the top of the crown. It is important that the leaves and tip of the crown are fully above the surface of the substrate, or they may rot off at the base.

Depending on the type of plant and its buoyancy, some plants may try to float up out of a lightweight substrate until the roots are settled. To keep the plant in place until it is strongly rooted, you can, temporarily, place a few rocks around the base. Remove them after a week or two and the plant will have a solid hold.

Epiphytic Plants

Some aquarium plants do much better if they are attached to a solid surface rather than planted in the substrate. *Anubias* species, *Bolbitis* species, and others like them will eventually reach their roots down into the substrate, while most ferns including Java fern will continue to feed from the water column and don't need the substrate at all. These are known as epiphytes.

Epiphytic plants may be sold in pots, bare-rooted, or pre-attached to rocks or wood. This last type of plant is typically substantially more expensive, and it is easy enough to do it yourself.

There are a few different ways to attach epiphytes to wood or rock. One method is to tie the plant on using cotton thread. Occasionally people suggest the use of fishing line. This is dangerous in a tank with any barbed fish, such as *Corydoras* or loricarid catfish. The fish can get tangled in the plastic fishing line and damage themselves badly, or even die. Dark cotton thread—black, brown, or green—is very unobtrusive in the tank and will eventually rot away. By then, the plant will have a secure hold on its perch. Cotton thread is one of the best ways to attach moss to branches.

A second method is to use plastic-coated wire plant ties (like the twist ties from bread bags, except brown or black in color). Plastic-coated wire is sold on rolls that can be cut to a suitable length and twisted around the plant. This method is sometimes easier than thread when trying to attach plants with large rhizomes, such as *Anubias*, to rounded rocks.

Using cotton thread to attach moss to rock. This same technique can be used for other epiphytes.

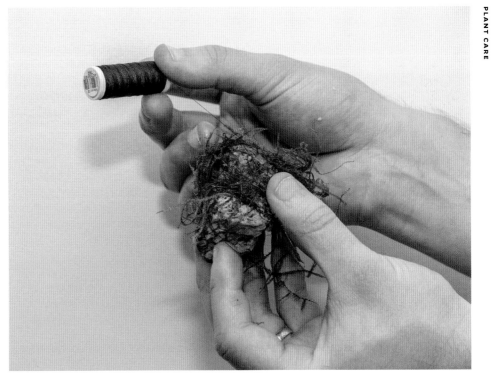

Using cotton thread to attach moss to wood.

A newer method of attaching epiphytes is to use the cyanoacrylate glue (brand name Super Glue) in gel form. Simply apply a small dab of glue to the wood or rock. Then press the roots of the plant into the gel. Hold for a moment (making sure to keep your fingers out of the way, because the glue will also bond skin), then place the glued plant in your tank. This type of glue allows you to get precise placement and make more complex plant groupings than might be possible with other methods.

Cyanoacrylate glue is also extremely useful for attaching moss to backgrounds or certain sections of large rocks. Put a small amount of glue on the rock, and then press the moss into it. The glue is also great for attaching *Bucephalandra* species to stone. These plants have small roots and don't like their rhizomes buried. Glue them to a small stone, set them where you want them, and the plant will grow down and around the stone, into the substrate. Cyanoacrylate gel works best on damp rock and can even be used under water, though it takes a bit more practice to use it this way.

Stem Plants

Stem plants are usually sold in bunches with a metal weight at the bottom. Occasionally they are also sold in in pots. When they are sold with a weight, it is very important to remove that weight as soon as possible. If you see that the stems below the weight are damaged, all is not lost; simply cut the stems off slightly above the weight in the nondamaged area.

Similarly, if the plants are potted, remove the pot and check the stems. Sometimes they are potted shortly before sale, and you can easily slip the whole mass of stems out of the rock wool. If the plants have rooted into the rock wool, there is no need to tease it all out, just cut the stems above the rock wool and abandon the old roots.

Stem plants do not need roots before planting. They will quickly establish new roots under good growing conditions, even if they have none when you get them. It is important to give each stem enough space to grow and receive light and nutrients without crowding. Use your finger to guide the stems down 2–3 inches into the substrate, then let the substrate close back around as you remove your hand. You don't need to plant each stem separately unless the stems are very thick (such as in *Ammania* species), but do not plant more than three stems together for best growth.

Just like crown plants, some kinds of stem plants, especially those with thick stems, are quite buoyant and may need help to stay in place until they have established some roots. This happens quite quickly, but until then, a small stone or two placed at the base of the plants can help keep them where they belong. These stones can be removed once the roots are established.

Stem plants, like many of the plants in this beautiful entry from The Art of the Planted Aquarium contest in Germany by Chris Helemann in 2010 are usually sold as bare-rooted bunches. However they produce strong roots quickly under good growing conditions.

Foregrounds and Tight Spaces

Foreground plants are sold potted, or on sheets of cocoa mat, or in packages of small *in vitro* plants. As we have discussed with other types of plants, potted foreground plants need to be very carefully removed from their pots. The problem is that it can be difficult to remove their tiny, delicate roots from the rock wool. If you need more than a few foreground plants, then those on cocoa mat sheets are a much better option. These plants can be gently peeled off their cocoa mat backing. If this is done carefully, the roots slide right out of the cocoa mat without damage.

No matter how the plants arrived, your foreground plants need to be divided into tiny individual sections and planted separately. Tedious as this task sounds, it will give each plug a chance to spread and grow, giving you a dense, attractive foreground much more quickly. If you try to plant larger patches, not only are the plants hard to get into the substrate, but they can only grow along the outer edge of each patch, taking a much longer time to fill in.

Divide foreground plants into very small sections.

Use pinsettes to plant tiny foreground plants or to plant stem plants in tight, hard-to-reach places.

Use the pinsettes to grasp each tiny group of plants by the roots. Slide the pinsettes below the surface of the substrate, then pull up and to the side, while letting go of the pressure on the roots. It may take some practice to perfect this technique, but it is well worth learning.

Pinsettes are also useful for planting stem plants in tight places, either in small tanks or between and behind rocks in a larger tank. The procedure is exactly the same as it is for the small foreground plants, except that you will want to get the stems deeper down into the substrate.

In vitro plants are becoming available in a greater variety and from more growers all the time. These are produced by Florida Aquatic Nurseries.

In Vitro Plants

In recent years, companies in Europe and Asia have been producing in vitro plants for aquarium use. We are lucky that these are now becoming more available in the United States also. These plants are cultured in a sterile environment, and sold in small, sealed packages with their roots in agar. There are a number of benefits of this type of plant. They are absolutely free of any algae, snails, or other pests. The plants are shelf-stable in just available light in shops for a very long time. This means that shop keepers have the opportunity to offer some plants that might be challenging for them to maintain in traditional aquarium shop conditions. Unlike many of the other plants sold in many of the big box pet stores, these in vitro plants are a wonderful value and can do well in your aquarium from the very beginning.

The only draw-back of some types of in vitro plants is that some can have very small roots in the beginning, making them difficult to plant in aquariums full of water. One of these species is the lovely *Pogostemon helferi*. A good method to take advantage of the benefits of these in vitro plants, and not get frustrated by short roots is the dry start method.

This simply means that you start with an aquarium where the substrate is wet, but there is no standing water. You plant your difficult plants, and then cover the tank with plastic to keep the humidity high. Uncover and recover the tank every day or so, just to make sure there is some air exchange, or else mold can develop. When the plants have rooted into the substrate well (usually two to four weeks after planting) the tank can be slowly and carefully filled. At that point, you are ready to enjoy your lovely plant carpet.

If you want to use some of these plants in a tank that is already established, the plants can be "dry started" in a smaller container, and then transplanted into your aquarium when they are large enough.

The in vitro plants come with their roots in agar, which must be carefully washed away under cool running water.

With small-rooted plants like these of *Pogostemon helferi*, it can be useful to use the dry start method to give the roots a chance to settle in. Start with your hardscape in place, and your substrate thoroughly saturated, but without much water sitting on the surface.

Plant your plants, making sure to keep them damp with a spray bottle.

Cover the tank with plastic wrap to keep the humidity high. Keep the tank covered for the next few weeks, but open it periodically to allow air exchange, or you can get fungus growing.

This was a small (6 gallon) nano tank, and without water in it, it is small enough and lightweight enough to move after planting. I planted it on the kitchen table, then moved it to its permanent home on top of a high file cabinet, and installed the light.

Make sure you keep everything nice and moist by spraying everything as needed. Do not let the plants dry out.

After three or four weeks your plants should be filling in nicely and will have established a good root system.

At that point, you can flood the tank by filling it very, very slowly with water. Your tank is now ready to be handled like any other tank.

TRIMMING AND DIVIDING AQUATIC PLANTS

Just as in the terrestrial garden, nothing is ever static in an aquatic garden. As plants grow, they will become too tall or too thick and require either trimming or division. You will also want to learn to trim your stem plants to make them bushy and full. One side benefit of all this trimming and dividing is that you will find that you soon have lots of extra plants to share with friends, trade with other aquatic gardeners or sell. Local independent aquarium shops are often happy to trade store credit for beautiful, locally grown plants, and some people even decide to sell or trade their excess plants on the internet.

Rhizome Plants

Rhizome plants, like Java fern (*Microsorum*), *Bolbitis*, and *Anubias*, can be divided by cutting anywhere along the length of the rhizome. I prefer to leave at least a couple of leaves on each section, and you can certainly leave more. These new divisions should be treated just like the parent plant and attached to a piece of wood or rock.

If you would like your *Anubias* to branch more, whether it is to fill out a section of your tank, or to produce more plants, you can do it without fully severing a section of the rhizome. Simply use a sharp knife or single-edged razor blade to nick the outer layer of the rhizome at spots where you would like a new branch to form.

Crown Plants

Many crown plants develop offsets at the base, and these can be cut away and replanted in different areas of the tank. *Echinodorus* species sometimes do this, but other times, the plant will just grow larger and larger to the point that it becomes unwieldy in the tank. In that case, remove the entire plant from the tank and divide the crown from top to bottom with a very sharp knife, making sure that each section contains both part of the leaves and part of the roots. Of course the divisions will look lopsided for a while, but before long, they will fill in and look like a lovely round plant again.

Echinodorus also send up bloom stalks quite frequently. If possibly, allow these bloom stalks room to get above the water level of the tank. The stalks will produce flowers and many will also produce small, fully functional plantlets. Allow these plantlets to stay on the stalk long enough to develop roots. Then cut the stalk on either side of the plantlets, and your baby plants are ready to go.

Stem Plants

Stem plants are among the easiest aquarium plants to propagate. In most species, it is as simple as cutting the tops off the stems and replanting. The majority of stem plants will regrow from the base stems, and the tops that have been removed can also be planted or rehomed. For the most part, aim to keep stem plants from spreading over the surface because when they do this, they block light to the plants below. They also reduce water motion on the surface of the tank, which can lead to algae problems.

To divide *Echinodorus* and many other crown plants, use a sharp knife to cut through the entire crown of the plant. ▶

The two (or more) sections of *Echinodorus* can then be planted separately. ◀

Some stem plants, such as many species of *Ludwigia* and *Myriophyllum*, branch readily underwater. The stand of plants gets wider and wider as it approaches the top of the water. These plants need to be thinned out regularly so that they don't take over the tank. Others stem plants grow more upright, and, if you want them to look fuller, require regular trimming to achieve that look.

A few species, such as *Rotala macrandra*, branch most prolifically if they are allowed to reach and spread along the surface of the water, so if you are interested in increasing your numbers of these plants, it can make sense to let them reach the surface and branch heavily before dividing them and replanting the branches. *Rotala macrandra* does not easily regrow from the base the way many stem plants do, so it is often necessary to let it branch naturally, trim the bottoms off and throw them away, then replant your full, branchy tops to make the stand larger.

Plants with Runners and Offsets

Some plants, like *Vallisneria* and many species of *Cryptocoryne*, reproduce via runners through the substrate. This makes propagation very easy: you simply cut the runners between plants and move them to their new homes. But this type of plant can also be a problem if the runners go into unintended areas and crowd out other plants. *Cryptocoryne* species are relatively slow growing, so this isn't much of a problem. *Vallisneria*, on the other hand, grows very rapidly. You will need to keep an eye out for new plants popping up in areas where you don't want them, and cut these runners as soon as you see them. Otherwise, you can end up with a tank full of nothing but *Vallisneria*!

Runner plants like this *Cryptocoryne* can be divided by cutting the runner between plants. Each individual can then be planted separately. ▶

The bulb plants, like *Crinum* species, *Nymphaea* species, and a few others reproduce by developing offset bulbs at the base of the plant. Many people never see this happen, because it requires excellent growing conditions and nutrient management for the plants to not only store enough nutrients in their own bulb, but to produce offsets as well. But hopefully you *are* going to provide excellent conditions for your plants, and in time, you may find that you have new, young plants growing up beside the parent plants. Don't be in a hurry to separate these young plants. Let them attain some size before you remove them.

PROPAGATING PLANTS BY SEED

Aponogetons are among the easiest plants to produce sexually. They often produce flowers in the aquarium. These flowers should be allowed to reach above the water surface. Then with a soft paintbrush, move the pollen around over the flowers.

Once pollinated, if the plant is a self-fertile species or hybrid, it will set seed. Place the seeds in a shallow container with fertile substrate, just barely covered with water. As the seeds germinate and the tiny plants grow, raise the depth of the water. When they are large enough, transfer them to your aquarium.

Aponogeton crispus seed.

9

WHILE IT IS NOT NECESSARY to house any animals in your planted tank, most people enjoy the color and movement fish and other creatures can bring to the aquarium. Let's face it: fish are the butterflies in our underwater gardens. There are a number of animals that can help you with housekeeping and are a useful addition to any tank as well.

There is a plethora of books on the subject of aquarium fish and invertebrates, and even more Web sites. There is no way I can touch on more than a few species in this book. However, I'd like to give you a starting point, with a few plant-safe, appropriately sized species. From there, do your homework. Learn about the species you are thinking of purchasing before you bring it home. Support your local independent aquarium shops as much as possible. In general, the owners of these shops are very knowledgeable about their animals and their care, and most are happy to share that knowledge with their clientele.

FISH AND ANIMALS TO AVOID

Learn to identify healthy fish versus sick ones. Fish with any spots or blemishes, those with clamped fins, or fish that sit and shimmy in one place rather than freely swimming around the tank are not healthy. Do not buy *any* fish out of a tank with even one sick fish, whether the others look healthy or not. The fish you choose should be plump, without any sign of a hollow belly. This is particularly true of species that are typically collected from the wild. These can make wonderful aquarium residents, and wild collection of freshwater fish, in

Thorichthys aureus, a beautiful cichlid, might look like a good choice for a large planted tank since it relatively peaceful and doesn't eat plants, but it digs and drops mouthfuls of substrate all over the plants. Unless a tank is carefully designed around its needs, you might not be happy with it in your aquatic garden.

general, is not harmful to the environment. But it can take a while for wild-caught fish to become acclimated. Let the shop keeper do this, and buy the fish once they have settled in. Many good independent shop keepers will allow you to reserve a specific number of fish in a tank to purchase after they have been in the store for a week or so.

It can be a little harder to identify unhealthy invertebrates (shrimp and snails are the types we mostly use in planted aquariums), but the water should be clean and smell fresh, and there should be no dead animals in the tank. Shrimp should be actively moving about the tank, picking at things and looking for things to eat. Shrimp do shed their exoskeleton from time to time, so don't confuse colorless shrimp skins sitting on the bottom with dead shrimp. This is a perfectly natural, healthy process.

Snails move much more slowly, but their shells shouldn't show any sign of erosion and, if possible, choose ones that are on the glass or moving around. Do *not* choose snails that are lying still, with the opening up, unless they have been knocked into that position in front of you. A healthy snail will try to right itself as soon as any danger is past.

Please don't buy fish just because they look pretty if you don't know how to care for them, and don't succumb to the Noah's ark mentality of fish keeping (two of these and two of those). Most fish are either solitary except while breeding, or live in large groups. It is rare for fish to live in pairs in the wild. While there are many beautiful and easy-to-care-for species, there are also species that can be tricky, needing very specific water conditions, a diet of live food, and so forth. Know what you are getting into and make sure that the conditions in your beautiful planted aquarium are compatible with the fish, as well as make sure the fish won't damage your plants. Pacu, for example, get too large for most home aquariums and will eat all the plants. While most people wouldn't consider purchasing grown fish, often there are cute babies available in pet stores. Beware!

Some fish, like silver dollars (*Mylossoma sp.*) and Buenos Aires tetras (*Hyphessobrycon anisitsi*), are vegetarians and will happily mow down all your plants, while others, like many of the larger loricarids (catfish family, especially the "plecos"), are just large and boisterous and can damage plants with their thrashing around. Still others, like many cave-spawning cichlids, some loaches, and the group of fish known as spiny eels, are diggers. If they don't actively dig up your plants, they will make a mess of the water as they burrow though your substrate.

A few fish fall in an in-between category of plant damage. Many Rift Lake cichlids are known to eat plants and also need water conditions different from those of most aquarium plants (very hard water and a high pH), but some of these fish can be successfully housed with certain tough, hardy plant species like *Anubias barteri* and Java fern (*Microsorum pteropus*).

Another type of fish that, in general, doesn't work well in planted tanks is goldfish. Yes, they are vegetarians, but the biggest reason people fail in keeping them with plants is that they choose tanks that are too small (each goldfish requires about 30 gallons of water) and they put the goldfish in first, and then try to add plants a few at a time. No wonder the fish think, "Salad bar!" If you feel that you must have goldfish in your planted tank, choose the largest tank you can afford, and plant it heavily with species that can grow faster than the fish can eat them, like *Vallisneria* and water sprite (*Ceratopteris thalictroides*), and tough plants that won't tempt them, like the ones suggested for Rift Lake tanks. Let these plants mature and start to grow fast. Then when the tank is doing really well, add your goldfish, making sure not to over stock the tank. Your goldfish may eat some plants, but if everything is healthy and growing, the damage they do will be offset by the plant growth.

Even Rift Lake cichlids can be housed in a planted tank if you choose both the fish and plant species carefully. This beautiful tank by Jan Ole Pedersen is the jewel in the center of a restaurant in Denmark.

I will introduce you mainly to the smaller fish suitable for planted aquariums for a couple of reasons. First, these smaller fish can be successfully kept in a wide range of tank sizes, but most newcomers to planted aquariums start with small to mid-sized tanks. Second, many of these smaller fish have similar and fairly simple husbandry requirements. The fish I introduce you to are not only pretty, hardy, and well suited to life in a planted tank. Most of the groups of fish mentioned below contain small species, but they also contain large ones and/or ones that will eat plants. So, once again, make sure you know what you are buying *before* you take it home.

Many fish, like Harlequin rasbora here, look better and behave more naturally when kept in large schools of the same species. Aquascape by Ghazanfar Ghori.

SCHOOLING FISH

In the wild, many fish live in schools with hundreds of individuals swimming together in tight formation. These range down to fish as small as 1/2 inch, so there is some type of schooling fish for all but the smallest tanks. Most schooling fish come from the general families of tetras, barbs, danios, and rasboras. All of these groups include very beautiful, colorful fish.

With all schooling fish, it is important to have enough of the same species that the fish feel comfortable. An absolute minimum would be six of the same species; a dozen or more is much better for most species. With most schooling fish, there are minimal differences in color or behavior between the sexes. In the few species where there are strong differences in color or finnage, it is best to have at least two or three females for each male. This way the males will show the best color, and any possible aggression will be spread among a larger group.

While it won't do the fish any harm to mix a number of compatible species in a tank of sufficient size, the fish will look best and behave most naturally with fewer species in larger groups. In a tank less than 4 feet long, a good plan would be to choose two or at most three species of narrow-bodied, faster-swimming schooling fish, and one species of larger-bodied slower-moving fish. In a 10- to 20-gallon tank, one fast-moving species and one slower, deep-bodied species would look better. Remember that you want the fish to be a colorful accent in your underwater garden. They should not take away from your beautiful plants. Too many fish, and it looks like a flock of starlings have taken over.

Tetras

Cardinal tetras (*Paracheirodon axelrodi*) are from the Amazon basin and are true jewels in the aquarium. Although they are small, these do best in a large school of two dozen or more. For this reason, a tank less than 3 feet long is probably not a good choice for them. They also show better schooling formation in a larger tank. Cardinal tetras are just one example of the many beautiful small tetras commercially available. Others with similar habits and needs, but different color patterns include black neons (*Hyphessobrycon herbertaxelrodi*) and glowlight tetras (*Hemigrammus erythrozonus*).

Cardinal tetra is highly sought after for its striking blue and red color bands.

Several small deep-bodied tetras are very beautiful. One of my favorites is the bleeding heart tetra (*Hyphessobrycon erythrostigma*). Other pretty ones include the red phantom tetra (*H. sweglesi*) and the black phantom tetra (*H. megalopterus*). These tetras can also be housed in a relatively small tank and do not need large numbers. A school of six to eight individuals is fine.

For tanks of 20 gallons or more, several slightly larger tetras can be beautiful additions. While these fish generally don't school quite as tightly as the smaller tetras, they still need a minimum of six to eight fish of the same species to feel comfortable. Colombian blue tetras (*Hyphessobrycon columbianus*) and diamond tetras (*Moenkhausia pittieri*) are two suggestions. Both of these species have the added advantage that they are not aggressive egg eaters, as many egg-scattering fish are. As long as there is plenty of plant cover in the tank, if you have a reasonable sized school of either species, it is likely that you will see babies (called "fry") showing up. If the fish are kept well fed, they will typically leave the fry alone and your school will increase over time.

Needing an even larger tank, the elegant Congo tetra (*Phenacogrammus interruptus*) is one of the most beautiful tetras available. It is not fast moving, but it does prefer to hang in a group of its own kind. A group of six or more is sufficient. Both sexes are pretty fish, but only the males develop long flowing fins as they mature.

Bleeding heart tetra is named for the distinctive red wedge-shaped spot on its side. ▲

Colombian blue tetra has a silvery bluish tinge to its body with red fins.

Congo tetras are calm fish that school beautifully in a larger aquarium.

Rasboras, Barbs, and Danios

The harlequin rasbora (*Trigonostigma heteromorpha*) and its close relative the lambchop rasbora (*T. espei*) are traditional favorites for planted aquariums. They are small and school in tight formation. While they still require a number of the same species to feel comfortable, they will be happy with fewer in their school than cardinal tetras.

There is a group of mid-sized barbs that are beautiful and are also useful for eating filamentous algae. Unfortunately, they are also likely to snack on fine-leaved plants, so you need to plan accordingly. If you want to include these fish, chose broad-leaved or tougher-leaved plants, and if the fine-leaved, delicate plant species are important to you, steer clear of the group. The rosy barb (*Pethia conchonius*), Odessa barb (*P. padamya*), and black ruby barb (*P. nigrofasciata*) are in this group.

There are many small danios available, and it seems more every day. They range from the old-fashioned zebra danio (*Danio rerio*) to the more recently introduced *Brachydanio kyathit* and my favorite, the glowlight danio (*Celestichthys choprae*). These fish display best in large schools, but will be perfectly healthy and happy in groups as small as five or six in a smaller tank.

Lambchop rasboras are named for the unique black marking on their side.

Odessa barb is an active swimmer that needs plenty of space in a tank for moving around. ▶

The zebra danio is named for its five dark blue stripes. ▼

LIVEBEARERS

Livebearers (fish that give birth to free-swimming offspring) are some of the easiest, most colorful, small aquarium fish. Some types have been bred in captivity for such a long time that many brightly colored varieties have been developed. Many of these fish make perfect first aquarium residents for a new aquatic gardener. They reproduce easily, which can be viewed as a positive or negative, depending on your desires.

If you want to watch your livebearers reproduce, it is best to stick to one variety of one species. Some species crossbreed, and *all* the different varieties within a species will crossbreed. The result is offspring that are not as nice as either set of parents.

There are some things to keep in mind before deciding to let livebearers reproduce. These fish display no parental care of the young at all. As soon as they are born, the young are looked upon as tiny bite-sized morsels to all the fish in the tank, including their own mother. If you can't stand this thought, you might be better off skipping reproduction. If you are willing to accept that a certain number of the babies (called "fry") will be eaten, you can still have a good number survive if you keep plenty of fluffy plants and/or floating plants with long roots in the tank for cover. In fact, if you become successful with your livebearer production, you can easily find yourself with too many. If they are a pretty variety, and you

Swordtails, whether they are wild species or colorful hybrids like these orange ones, can make a stunning display in a larger tank. Swordtails are named for the elongated rays on the caudal (tail) fin.

can grow them out to a nice size, some local aquarium stores may be willing trade them for store credit. You can also sell them through local aquarium club auctions.

For tanks of 20 gallons or larger, swordtails like *Xiphophorus helleri* and its hybrids are stunning tank residents. At up to 4 inches long, they are a good-sized, fast-swimming fish, and need some room to move around. They come in a wide variety of colors from green to red to velvety black, so there is a swordtail to fit all tastes. The males can be a bit quarrelsome if they don't have enough females around to keep their interest, so it is best to keep them in a ratio of one male to two or three females. Females are just as colorful as males, but don't have the long tail extension of their male counterparts.

If your tank is a bit smaller, 10 gallons or larger, platys (*Xiphophorus maculatus* and *X. variatus*) have an even wider array of colors than the swordtails do, are more peaceful and a quite a bit smaller. Male platys are much more gentle than swordtails, so there is less need to spread things out among a larger number of females.

Males and females are colored exactly the same, but they can be easily sexed by the shape of their anal fin. In the female, this is a normal fin. In the males, the anal fin is modified into a tubular fin called a gonopodium, used for reproduction. (This is true for swordtails and guppies also, but those livebearers also have other traits that make sexes easy to determine.)

If you want your platys to reproduce, of course get both sexes. If you want to enjoy them without dealing with babies, get a group of males. Then you can enjoy a variety of colors without worrying about crossing them. You might think that buying a group of females would work, but unless the females have been kept strictly separate from males from very early in life, they are probably already pregnant by the time you buy them, and you'll end up with babies anyway.

And yes, for even smaller tanks, there are still appropriate livebearers. Guppies (*Poecilia reticulata*) come in a dazzling array of colors. They are small, peaceful fish, and although males may do a lot of posturing, there is rarely any serious fighting among them. While females may have some color in their tail fins, it is the males who are the peacocks in this species. Guppies breed like rabbits, so if you have fish of both sexes, you must be ready for that, but you can purchase a lovely group of males for a small tank and enjoy all the color without any of the fuss.

Even tinier is the Endler's livebearer (*Poecilia wingei*). I have included this scientific name here, as it is the best we have, but there is still debate whether this is a separate species from regular guppies (*P. reticulata*). The two types of fish can and will happily interbreed, so please do not keep them together. Endler's, which are closer to their wild predecessors, are smaller in size than most domestic guppies, and the females have even less color, being a rather solid gray with a lighter belly.

In the past few years, aquarists have selectively bred a number of different color varieties of Endler's so there is a good deal of choice here too, though their tails are neither as large nor as colorful as those of most male guppy varieties. A 7-gallon tank or larger is fine for a small colony of these pretty little fish. They are also not quite as prolific as domestic guppies, so are less likely to overrun your tank in short order.

SIAMESE FIGHTING FISH

I would be remiss to leave out Siamese fighting fish (*Betta splendens*), which is so often mistreated, both by pet stores and by the uneducated public. Bettas are not aggressive fish unless two males are kept in the same container together. Even that behavior has mostly been bred in by people, as these fish were originally developed for fighting like cock fighting and dog fighting. Although this unfortunate practice still goes on in the Far East, the fighters are short-finned varieties of the fish we see in pet stores. The ones sold to the general public for aquarium use have been bred for their beautiful bright colors and lovely fins. In pet stores they are often displayed in very small containers, at room temperature. This is *not* an acceptable way to maintain these fish once you get them home. Furthermore, most of the betta bowls and other small containers are not appropriate for this purpose.

Siamese fighting fish are known for their beautiful bright colors and lovely fins.

Bettas come from a very warm part of the world, and they do not do well in unheated aquariums. They are happiest at temperatures of at least 78°F. They also are much happier with room to swim and with quiet, inoffensive tank mates who will not nip at their long fins. Male bettas do beautifully in a planted nano tank of 5 gallons by themselves or in a larger tank if careful thought is given to their tank mates. Alternatively, a group of females, who come in beautiful colors but have short fins, can be housed together in a tank of 20 gallons or more.

While it is possible to breed bettas at home in a tank with plenty of floating plants, you would need to have a second tank to move the female to after she has bred. The male will vigorously defend his floating bubble nest and may harm the female in the process if she doesn't have enough room to get away.

FISH FOR THE NANO TANK

While I have already mentioned a few species that can be used in small planted aquariums, there are some other species of fish that are so small that they get lost in larger tanks, and are at risk from larger tank mates. These species make the perfect inhabitants for small tanks, in the range of 7 to 15 gallons. It is important to be aware that these small tanks with fish in them require great attention to detail to keep the fish healthy and the tanks free of problem algae.

A male celestial pearl danio (shown here) is more brightly colored than a female, but both have starlike spots all over their body.

Scarlet badis have bright red vertical stripes on their sides that are clearly visible on males (shown here). The females, in comparison, are a drab grayish brown.

Ember tetras are one of the smallest tetras available. At less than ½ inch long, their bright orangey-red glow is responsible for their common name. They are good schooling fish and are comfortable in groups as small as 8 to 12 individuals, so are well suited to tanks of 7 gallons or larger.

A very popular nano fish species is the celestial pearl danio, *Celestichthys margaritatus*. This incredibly beautiful little fish needs to be kept in groups of 10 or more, and without larger fish that might frighten it. For this reason, celestial pearl danios are a good option for tanks of 7 to 15 gallons that can be devoted to their care. These fish sometimes come into the stores quite thin, in which case they will need some careful nurturing and small frequent feedings to get them up to healthy weight. Celestial pearl danios need the company of others of their kind, and you will often observe fin flaring and sparring among the males. They do not school as tightly as many other species do.

Another popular nano fish is *Boraras brigittae*. This little fish is brightly colored, schools well, and is not as fragile as its tiny size would suggest. As long as it is housed with species that will not look at it as a prey item and as long as it is in a school of eight or more individuals, it is an easy fish to keep.

For unheated small tanks, the perfect choice is the white cloud mountain minnow, *Tanichthys albonubes*. This beautiful little temperate water fish is extremely hardy, but does not show well in a large community tank. In a small tank with a good sized group of the same species, this fish is a true gem.

The scarlet badis (*Dario dario*) is a stunning little fish that does beautifully in a nano tank. The color of the males is second to none, although the female is not colorful and often overlooked. These are peaceful, but not schooling fish. If possible, try to obtain females for your males so that you can watch their courtship displays. A pair or trio (one male and two females) in a 7-gallon tank, or four to six fish in a 10-gallon tank will get along fine. The one problem with scarlet badis is that they are micropredators, and will happily hunt down and eat any baby shrimp in your tank. So they are not good candidates for a shrimp tank.

"HELPER" FISH

Some fish are helpful in dealing with algae problems in the planted tank. They should not be used as the primary method to control algae—that should be left to good management and regular large water changes—but these fish can be a useful part of your overall algae management program.

Otocinclus catfish are excellent for eating up diatoms (sometimes called brown algae), which appear as a fine, powdery, brown substance on plants and equipment in your tank. These tiny catfish are almost always wild caught and sometimes arrive in poor condition. Wait until they have been in the store for a week or two and are healthy, have nice round bellies, and are eating well before you bring them home. *Otocinclus* catfish do best in a school of 12 or more individuals. In a very small tank, you could have fewer catfish, but never have less than three in a tank.

Bushy nosed plecos (*Ancistrus* spp.) are small, sucker-mouthed catfish that can be helpful in removing green algae from the glass and from leaf surfaces. Many people love them in their planted tanks, but certain individuals can be troublesome, rasping holes in the leaves of broad-leaved plants, especially *Echinodorus* species.

A number of fish are useful in cleaning up filamentous green algae in the aquarium, if it isn't out of control. Florida flag fish (*Jordanella floridae*), rosy barb (*Pethia conchonius*), or Odessa barb (*Pethia padamya*) are good choices to help keep algae at bay. You will sometimes hear mollies (*Poecilia* spp.) suggested as good fish for control of filamentous algae. While it is true that they will eat filamentous algae, these fish come from areas with either brackish or very hard water. As such, water conditions that are best for them are generally not best for a planted tank.

A Word about Catfish

You will sometimes hear various catfish referred to as "cleaner fish." Other than *Otocinclus* and *Ancistrus*, very few catfish are great algae eaters, and many have specialized needs. They are wonderful fish in their own right, and if you are interested in them, by all means learn more about them. Many of the smaller species can be right at home in a planted tank. But don't buy them thinking that they will be animated vacuum cleaners and take care of "fish poop" or overfeeding problems in your aquarium. Catfish need and deserve exactly the same thought and care as any other fish that you choose for your aquarium.

Siamese algae eaters have a black lateral stripe along their side, but so do several other, similar-looking species. Make sure you get the right fish.

Banded garra is a peace-loving algae eater.

For many years now, it has been known that Siamese algae eater was one of the few animals that would eat black brush algae. This species is one of several very similar fish in the genus *Crossocheilus*. It appears that the "true" Siamese algae eater is probably *C. langei*, however, there are a number of very similar species for sale. This may account for some of the stories we hear of some Siamese algae eaters seeming aggressive and nippy in some tanks, while other, very similar looking fish are totally inoffensive. In any case, there are other problems with this fish, regardless of its scientific name.

Siamese algae eaters are much more efficient algae eaters when they are small and hungry. Once they learn about fish food, they are much happier to have you provide for them than to go scrounging for algae. They also grow quite large, to about 6 inches in length and are happiest in groups. That means they are not good candidates for smaller tanks. They are also determined jumpers, so the tank must have a close fitting hood or you are liable to find the fish dried up on the floor.

More recently, another fish has come on the scene that is a much better choice for eating black brush algae. That is *Garra flavatra*, sold under a number of fanciful common names ranging from rainbow garra and butterfly garra to the perhaps more appropriate banded garra. This species grows to a more moderate 3½ inches and is absolutely peaceful with other fish in the aquarium. Banded garras seem to enjoy being in a group of their own kind and when kept in such a group will cavort around the tank together. They are excellent algae eaters in general, but will go to work on black brush algae as nothing else will.

INVERTEBRATES

A number of invertebrate animals can be useful and beautiful additions to the planted aquarium. In fact, ornamental shrimp keeping has become a hobby of its own. For aquatic gardeners with tanks smaller than 7 gallons, it is best to avoid fish altogether. In small tanks, invertebrates, including the colorful small shrimp available, put less strain on the biological processes in the tank with their smaller size and still give some life and color in the tank.

Nothing brightens an aquarium like a bright red cherry shrimp. And they are great algae eaters too!

Shrimp

Several brightly colored shrimp are available currently. *Neocaridina heteropoda* is a species that has been bred to include many different color varieties. The easiest to keep are the old-fashioned cherry shrimp, which, as you can probably guess, are bright red. But there are also yellow, orange, and even blue varieties available. In general, the females are more colorful than the males. They reproduce quite easily in the aquarium, but keep in mind that if you mix members of the same genus, even if they are different colors, they will interbreed, and your offspring will not keep the pretty, distinct colors of their parents. Start with about eight individuals of mixed sexes and you will have a pretty, interesting, and undemanding colony.

Another type of shrimp that is beautiful and fairly easy to keep is the bee shrimp, *Caridina cantonensis*. This little black- or brown-striped creature is among the first type of ornamental shrimp kept by aquarists and is quite simple to keep. This species can be mixed with *Neocaridina* shrimp without fear of interbreeding.

From the bee shrimp was bred the wildly popular crystal red shrimp. It has red and white stripes instead of the brown and whitish stripes of the wild type. These shrimp are graded based on the amount and quality of the red and white stripes. Crystal red shrimp are a little more sensitive than the original species, so try your hand at easier shrimp first, but the beauty of the crystal reds is very tempting, and if you learn to raise them well, they can be very rewarding. Their prices range from quite reasonable for pretty but low-grade shrimp to unbelievably expensive for the highest grade individuals. Honestly, my preference is for the lower grade shrimp, so don't let "fancy" prices stop you.

Selectively bred from the same wild species that has gave us the cherry shrimp, the yellow shrimp is greatly sought after by aquarists for its unique color.

An extremely popular shrimp species that is also an important "worker" animal in your aquarium is *Caridina multidentata*, also known as Amano shrimp, after Takashi Amano, the aquascaping master who introduced them. Amano shrimp are larger than most of the ornamental shrimp and are very good at eating filamentous algae in aquariums. I keep at least a couple in every tank and quite a few in larger tanks. Unfortunately, they rarely reproduce in the home aquarium, as the newborn baby shrimp of this species requires a period of time in brackish water in nature. Unlike other types of shrimp that will happily colonize your tank without help from you, Amano shrimp will only increase as you purchase them and introduce them to your tank.

Bamboo shrimp (*Atyopsis moluccensis*) is another interesting inhabitant for the planted tank. When full grown, this species is much larger than the others mentioned, but it is completely inoffensive and will not bother plants, fish, or other shrimp. These shrimp are filter feeders and use the "fans" on their first appendages to sift tiny bits of food out of the water. If they are very hungry, they will get down on the substrate and sift what bits they can find there, but this is a sign that you need to feed them better. Well-fed, healthy bamboo shrimp will station themselves high in the tank, in the flow from the filter. To make sure they are well fed, crush some of your fish food to a powder as you feed the fish. The shrimp will filter the particles out of the water as it passes by.

Bee shrimp has dark stripes and a fairly translucent body.

The amount and quality of the red and white stripes in crystal red shrimp varies and has led to the establishment of a grading system.

Snails

Some people hate snails in their planted tanks, others love snails, and a third group is somewhere in the middle. There are many snails that are neither good nor bad in a planted tank unless you find them unsightly. These include Malaysian trumpet snails (*Melanoides tuberculata*), which burrow in the substrate, pond snails (in the family Lymnaeidae) that are sometimes inadvertently introduced with plants, and ramshorn snails (mostly in the family Planorbidae), which people sometimes choose to introduce and then find that they proliferate too quickly.

You will sometimes hear people saying that these snails are eating their plants. The fact is that snails don't eat healthy plant tissue. If you see snails munching on a leaf, it is because the leaf is already dead or dying. Most of the time when these snails become a nuisance, it is due to overfeeding the tank. When you cut back on the amount of food introduced into the tank, the snail numbers will decrease also. If you still have too many snails, introduce a few small loaches like the zebra loach (*Botia striata*) or yoyo loach (*B. almorhae*). The loaches will take care of the snails for you.

There is also a type of snail, the assassin snail (*Clea helena*) which eats other snails. It can be amusing to watch the low speed chase of an assassin snail tracking down its prey, but my experience is that you need a lot of them to clear a big snail infestation.

Nerite snails (*Neritina* spp.) are interesting and useful planted tank residents. They are effective eaters of diatoms and will make some headway on other types of algae. Unfortunately, in exchange for eating algae, they lay white eggs all over the place that can be difficult to remove. The eggs do not hatch, since this is another animal that needs brackish water for reproduction, but they can be unsightly. Still with all the colors, patterns, and shapes available among the genus, these snails are definitely worth considering.

Other snails that you may see in pet stores include apple snails, or mystery snails, which are large snails from several different species in the family Ampullariidae. These snails are *not* safe for a planted aquarium and will quickly turn your tank into their personal salad bar. The Colombian ramshorn snail (*Marisa cornuarietis*), which is not closely related to the smaller ramshorns, is also herbivorous and should not be introduced into your planted tanks. In general, the only larger snails that can be safely introduced to the planted aquarium are nerites.

FEEDING YOUR ANIMALS

Feeding your fish is a balancing act with or without plants. You must feed enough to keep your fish healthy, but not so much that there are leftovers which can foul the water. In a planted tank, too much food can lead to unsightly algae problems. The exact amount to feed will vary depending on the number and size of fish in the tank. It is far more common for people to overfeed their fish than for them to let fish starve to death.

Keep in mind that the stomach of a fish is approximately the size of its eye. That's pretty small. In a planted tank, there is also a constant small supply of food in the form of the biofilm that develops on the plants. And if you have algae-eating fish, you want them to concentrate on algae, not be looking for a hand-out all the time.

Your staple food can be a good quality dried flake food. If you have fish that feed at the bottom of the tank, you might also find that a small sinking pellet food can be useful. If you keep shrimp, make sure to feed only food that does not contain copper. Copper is added to some fish food as a parasite preventative, but it is extremely toxic to invertebrates.

Besides a dry food staple diet, your fish will appreciate occasional supplementation with frozen foods like brine shrimp and blood worms. These should be rinsed thoroughly under tap water as you thaw them in a brine shrimp net before feeding. This will remove any nutrient-laden liquid that can cause algae problems for your tank, and which the fish can't eat. An even greater treat if you can find it is live brine shrimp and black worms. Some shops do sell these and again, these foods should be rinsed before serving, but your fish will go wild for them and show you their brightest colors.

Feed only the amount of food that your fish can clean up in about one minute. In a planted tank, feeding once a day is fine, and it will not hurt your fish in the least to miss a day here or there, or even a weekend if you go away.

We all go on vacation from time to time, and unlike most furry pets, your aquarium fish can get by with very little care. If you will be gone for less than a week, feed your fish well for a week or two before you leave, do a large water change two days before, and they will be fine with no outside care while you are gone. If you will be away for more than a week, ask someone to stop by twice a week and just check on things. Do not leave it up to your caregiver to guess the amount of food. More tanks have been ruined by overfeeding during vacation than any other way I know.

You can also purchase automatic feeders and pre-load them, but these units are expensive and prone to failure if there is humidity in the air, as damp food gets stuck in the feeder. I do know people who use and like these devices, but I have never felt the need to invest in them. I also would not recommend the vacation food blocks that slowly dissolve, releasing a little food at a time. There is no good way of regulating these, and you don't know that all of your fish will find or understand the feeding system.

10

AQUA-SCAPING STYLES

A ESTHETICALLY PLEASING AQUASCAPES don't just happen. They have to be set up and planted with care. Before we look at the various aquascape styles common today, we need to review some basic design principles.

DESIGN PRINCIPLES

Tried-and-true design principles are used by artists in all genera. These principles are just as important to aquascaping as they are to any other form of art. As you become more adept at aquascaping, you can certainly push the boundaries or even break these "rules," but until you have a good feeling for what you are doing, it's better to keep them in mind.

The first and possibly most important principle is the "rule of thirds," which says that you should try to put focal points approximately one third of the way from one end or the other, and one third of the way from back to front. These are the strongest points in your layout and will draw the eye in the most pleasing way.

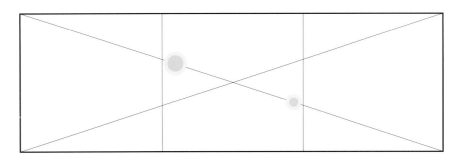

The golden intersections (see dots) are the strongest places for focal points in a tank. ▶

Even in this small casual tank, the maker, Kaylan Bhowmick, has divided the space visually into a low foreground, a mid-height middle ground, and a taller background. He has also used a nice assortment of leaf colors, sizes, and shapes. Aquascape by Kaylan Bhowmick. ▼

Just as it is important to place focal points on the thirds, it is also important to divide a tank roughly into thirds from front to back. Plant low-lying foreground plants toward the front of the tank or use a plain substrate foreground. In the middle of the tank place plants and hardscape of middle height, and in the back of the tank, arrange your tallest plants. While not all styles of tank (notably Dutch tanks) are designed around hardscape, for the home aquarium, a tank with a strong mid-ground hardscape will be the easiest to maintain and keep looking beautiful for a long time.

It is also important to use a variety leaf sizes, colors, and textures in your design. That doesn't mean you can't have a beautiful tank using only green plants; you can as there are many different tones of green among aquatic plants.

Be careful when introducing accent colors into your tank. While some people enjoy lots of red plants in their aquascapes, I prefer that red plants be used as a lovely pop of color rather than fighting with each other for dominance.

This is a good example of a concave aquascape. Aquascape by Pedro Rosa.

There are a few main shapes to keep in the back of your mind when designing an aquascape. In a sloping layout, plants and hardscape are lower on one side of the tank and higher on the other side. The slope can be from right to left or vice versa.

In a concave layout, the planting is lower in the middle and higher on both sides. This leaves a nice open V- or U-shaped space in the center of the tank. It is not necessary for the landscape to be equally high on both sides.

In the convex style, the layout is higher in the middle and then tapers down on both sides. Again, this does not need to be exactly symmetrical.

.The island style, as its name implies, has an island of planting, generally created with hardscape, in the middle of the tank, with no plants around it. Generally, this layout uses clean white sand around the island to really contrast with the planted area, though occasionally you see an island layout done with darker sand or gravel.

Whatever style you choose, your tank will usually look better with some negative space—an area with no plants. Negative space can be an area of exposed substrate, an area where the back of the tank is exposed, or both. Some people like to include a path through the tank as negative space and to add depth to the layout.

Filipe Olivera has created a sloping design with a whimsical tree in this lovely aquascape. Aquascape by Filipe Olivera.

Convex aquascapes can be very attractive, too. Aquascape by Filipe Olivera.

The dark substrate in this island-style layout by Oliver Knott contrasts nicely with the bright green foliage of *Pogostemon helferi*.

Negative space is important to a good aquascape. Can you imagine this tank if the maker had plants running right to the surface, all along the back? It wouldn't have near the impact that this fantastic aquascape does. Aquascape by Luis Carlo Galarraga.

HARDSCAPE MATERIALS

The hardscape could be considered the bones of your planted aquarium. It is the hard, nonliving materials in your tank. Chosen and placed well, the hardscape gives longevity to the layout. Plants in front of or behind the hardscape can be changed many times if you choose, giving a fresh new look to the tank without doing a major rework to the aquascape. Wood and rock of various sorts are the most common hardscape materials with people who are serious about aquascaping, but some people branch out and include man-made decorative materials in their tank.

Stone

Many types of stone are suitable for the aquarium. You can buy nice stone at most independent aquarium shops and online. Some of the more common types of rock commercially available are lava rock, Texas holey rock (a limestone rock with holes from a specific region in Texas), pagoda stone (a dense solid rock with a flat base), petrified wood, and slate. You can purchase the highly desirable dragon stone (a soft rock with creases and crevices), manten stone (from mountains in Japan), and others from stores that specialize in aquascaping. Some of these stores ship products, also. This can be expensive if you have a large tank, though.

It is also entirely possible to use locally collected stone for your tank that costs nothing but some time and effort on your part. Most stone that doesn't crumble or break easily by hand is suitable for aquarium use. Avoid rocks that have any metal in them, as this can leach into the water.

Some aquarists prefer to avoid calcium carbonate-bearing rock because, over time, this type of rock can raise the hardness in a tank. However, you should be doing large, regular water changes, and if you are, you won't have any problem with a build-up of minerals. I regularly use seiryu stone, which is a calcium carbonate-bearing rock, and have no problems with it at all. If you feel that you must avoid calcium carbonate-bearing rock, you can test by putting a few drops of muriatic acid (available from the hardware store for cleaning concrete floors) on the stone. If the stone contains calcium carbonate, it will fizz in reaction to the acid. Be sure to use gloves and safety glasses when handling muriatic acid, and work in a well-ventilated area.

Good places to collect rocks are at road cuts along the highway or anywhere heavy equipment has done the hard work of exposing the stone for you. My husband cringes when I ask him to pull into a rest stop at a road cut, knowing that the back of our pick-up truck will soon be full of more rock. Rivers and beaches can be a good place to find water-smoothed stones. These non-textured stones don't work for all aquascapes, but can be useful for some. Old stone walls on abandoned farm land (don't take stone from a wall that is in use) and abandoned quarries can be other easy sources.

You will find markedly different types of rock in different parts of the country, so keep your eyes open on road trips. Particularly look for rock with a lot of character in the form of crevasses, cracks, and other surface texture. Just be careful not to collect rocks in state or national parks, and if you are on private land, be polite and ask first. To prepare the stone for your tank, scrub off any surface dirt with a wire brush and rinse thoroughly.

If you really get interested in aquascaping, it pays to keep your used or potentially useful stones either in piles (by type) in a corner of the yard or in plastic tubs in your basement. The more choices you have to work with, the more you can let your creativity go.

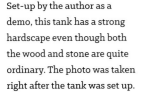

Set-up by the author as a demo, this tank has a strong hardscape even though both the wood and stone are quite ordinary. The photo was taken right after the tank was set up.

Wood

Wood is a very popular hardscape material for the planted aquarium. As with stone, you can purchase a number of good options from many local independent aquarium shops, and there are good sources online too.

While some people use found wood in the aquariums, doing so is chancier than with stone. You need to find well-seasoned hard wood and also know what kind of wood it is. Some wood types are safe in aquariums, while others deteriorate quickly when submerged, or release sap or tannin that causes problems in the confined space of an aquarium. I would not advise collected wood for a new aquarist.

Among the commercially available types of wood, manzanita is a big favorite. This very hard wood holds up well for a long time under water. It is often branchy, with beautiful, graceful shapes. Spider wood is another favorite, often available commercially. It starts with a nice reddish color, though, like all wood, it tends to blacken with prolonged submersion. Both of these types of wood (and many others) require soaking before they will sink if the pieces are large.

Lightweight driftwood like the pieces in this tank will hold up better if waterproofed with epoxy or spar varnish first.

Soaking can be done in a clean plastic trash barrel or other container large enough to keep the wood fully submerged. If necessary, place some large rocks on the wood to hold it down until it is fully waterlogged. The water should be changed at least weekly in the soaking container to allow any tannin to leach from the wood. You may see white fuzz forming on the wood as it soaks. This is a harmless fungal overgrowth that will run its course and die off. If you use wood in the aquarium that has not been pre-soaked (we sometimes do this with thin pieces that can be wedged between stones to prevent floating), don't panic if you see this fuzz. The fish will pick at it, and it will disappear with time. It's harmless.

Malaysian driftwood and Mopani wood from Africa have the advantage that they need no soaking to get them to sink. However, both leach large quantities of tannins into the tank water if not pre-soaked. The tannins are not dangerous to either your plants or fish, but turn the water a clear but brownish color. Some people don't mind this, but most do a number of water changes and/or use activated carbon in their filters to remove this coloration. The leaching process can last several months, depending on the thickness of the wood. Mopani wood comes in interesting shapes, though it is coarse looking to my tastes, while Malaysian driftwood is often just unattractive wooden chunks.

Aquascaping doesn't have to be serious, as this tank by Oliver Knott shows. It's up to you. If you want to play, have fun.

Manufactured Materials

While my preference is for the natural materials listed above, there is nothing to say that you have to stick to natural materials. If you want a sunken ship or a castle in your aquarium, go for it. This is your tank, no one else's, and you should enjoy it.

Oliver Knott, one of the most famous aquascape artists in Europe, believes in playful tanks and sometimes uses surprising materials. He has created wonderful tanks with jungle animals, "Minions," and even a complete soccer field.

Just be sure that materials you choose are aquarium safe, by either purchasing items meant for aquariums, or choosing items that will not break down under water. Any stone materials can be tested just like natural stone, with a drop of muriatic acid.

Backgrounds

It is very popular at present to leave the back of the aquarium uncovered, allowing the viewer to see straight through the tank. This can be very effective, making the tank look like a living jewel depending on where it sits. If your tank is against a plain color wall, this might be exactly the look you want, but many times, a home tank is in a place where you don't want to see what's behind it.

The simplest solution when you don't want to see through a tank is to purchase a rolled aquarium backing that can be taped to the back of the tank. Almost every aquarium store sells these. The backings often have some underwater scene on one side, and on the other side a plain black or deep blue. I strongly recommend that you resist the urge to put the "scene" side on your tank. It will just detract from your beautiful aquatic garden as it starts to grow in. My preference is for a black background, but go for the blue if you like it.

If you are sure that you will always want the back of your aquarium to be the same color, you can spray paint it after carefully masking off the rest of the tank. Obviously, you'd want to do this outdoors while the tank is still empty.

Another beautiful option, though more complicated, is to put a piece of translucent plexiglas behind the tank, then fix a light, either fluorescent or LED, behind that, so that it glows through. You can get really lovely effects with this method.

There are other options as well. Some people attach silicone cork to the inside of the aquarium and cover that with epiphytic plants like Java fern, *Anubias*, and mosses. There are pre-made tank inserts that simulate rockwork or tree trunks. Some of these inserts are fairly lifelike, but the better ones are very expensive. Finally, there are some lovely aquarium systems where all the tank equipment—filter, pump, heater, and so—is behind a false, black wall on the back of the tank. These tanks give a really sleek, polished look to the aquascape, with no equipment showing at all.

STYLE CHOICES FROM JUNGLE TO ZEN GARDEN

Just as with terrestrial gardening, there are many choices in terms of designing your aquatic garden. Some people enjoy a seat-of-the-pants approach, trying a little bit of everything, as they learn which plants work best for them. Other people like to put more structure and planning into their garden design, with a specific end in mind. As the art of the planted aquarium has matured, several different "schools" have developed, as well as tanks that borrow from a number of different schools and others that break all the rules entirely. It's up to you.

Dutch Aquarium

The Dutch can be credited with the first carefully designed planted aquariums in the 1930s. Over the years, NBAT, the national aquarium group of the Netherlands, has established strict judging criteria for this style of tank, which includes the use of a certain number of plant species, which must be arranged in specific ways so that they create a feeling of great depth in the tank.

Dutch aquascapes are heavily dependent on stem plants, and these must be trimmed and replanted regularly to keep each stem at the proper height. While other forms of aquascaping depend heavily on hardscape, this element is not an important part of a Dutch aquarium. If rocks and wood are used at all, they must not, in any way, upstage the plants themselves.

A true Dutch tank is part of this home. Even the cabinet is considered part of the total design and complements the home's furnishings. Aquascape by Willem von Wezel.

The back and side walls of a Dutch-style aquarium are completely hidden by plants, either in front of the walls, or by actually attaching epiphytic plants on cork or other surfaces to hide the glass. Other important aspects of the Dutch aquarium are use of the golden intersection design principle (see illustration 189), the use of streets of plants that lead the eye through the aquascape, and varying textures and colors of the plants.

Besides the aquascaping done inside the tank, a true Dutch aquarium is also beautifully presented with lovely furniture-quality cabinetry. Even the way it is placed in the room and how it is viewed is taken into consideration in judging these tanks. Unfortunately, in recent years, the true Dutch aquascape has been supplanted by other styles. It's not uncommon to find on the internet any tank with a lot of stem plants and lots of color being called a "Dutch aquarium," but it is not a true Dutch aquarium unless its meets all the criteria above.

Nature Aquarium

The term "Nature aquarium" was coined by the great Japanese nature photographer and aquascape master, Takashi Amano. His books can be credited with popularizing planted aquariums in a way that had never been seen before. Amano's Nature aquarium style seeks not to imitate a natural underwater scene, but to evoke the same feelings in a person as can be felt when out in nature.

Dutch aquascapes typically include a "plant street" as seen here. Aquascape by Marlene Reejwijk.

Unlike the Dutch aquarium, the Nature aquarium depends heavily on a strong hardscape, the rocks and/or wood that become the bones of the aquascape. While the plants used can vary greatly, the foreground and midground areas of the tank tend to be planted with species that can go for longer periods without excess pruning. If stem plants that require regular, heavy pruning are used, they are typically toward the back of the tank. But often, Nature aquarium tanks will have no stem plants and will be simple arrangements of slow-growing plants like *Anubias*, Java ferns, and mosses.

Where Dutch tanks usually are filled with plants from one end to the other, there are rarely any plants attached to the glass in a Nature aquarium style tank. The back glass is often left clear or it might be covered with black or a frosted material. Carefully planned open space or areas where there are no plants at all is as important to the overall design as where the plants are placed.

Many well-designed Nature aquarium style tanks can be maintained with a minimum of fuss over a long period and they are a calm, beautiful highlight in any room. For these reasons, the style has become extremely popular.

Diorama Aquarium

An off-shoot of the Nature aquarium movement has been the Diorama aquarium. This style tank seeks to reproduce terrestrial scenes in great detail within an aquarium. In this category you will find sweeping mountain ranges, intimate wooded glens, waterfalls, and seashores. I've occasionally even seen Stonehenge and a Hobbit hole recreated.

Diorama tanks can be very rewarding to produce for a contest, but most of them would be a lot of work to maintain long-term. Certainly once you've got your plant growing skills down give it a try if this style speaks to you. It can be a lot of fun.

Biotope Aquarium

For those who are very interested in natural water systems, a biotope aquarium might be just the thing. Biotope aquariums have a small but very enthusiastic following worldwide, and contests for this type of tank are fiercely competitive. This type of aquarium is also a wonderful way to introduce children to nature, either in a classroom or as a family project.

The biotope tank should seek to recreate a small slice of a natural water system in a specific part of the world. It could be a little stream in a corner of Thailand, a tributary of the Río Negro in Brazil, or even a pond bank near your home. In fact, often the most successful biotope tanks contain plants, animals, and hardscape that are collected locally where the aquarist can actually observe the natural biotope in person.

This stunning tank is a wonderful example of the Nature aquarium style introduced by Takashi Amano. It has a very natural feel, with a strong stone hardscape and lovely, flowing planting. Aquascape by Luis Carlos Galarraga.

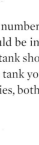

If you choose a biotope from another part of the world, there are a number of internet sites than can help you decide exactly what plants and animals should be included and what the biotope looks like. It is good to remember that your biotope tank should look, to as great an extent as possible, like a slice of nature, just the size of the tank you are using. For this reason, biotope tanks typically have a limited number of species, both in terms of plants and animals, unless it is a very large tank.

Fusion-style Aquarium

For lack of a better term, I'll call tanks that borrow a bit from several of the above styles Fusion style. Sometimes this sort of tank has a tendency to turn into a Jungle-style tank if it is not kept in check. This is the style that most people, especially novice aquatic gardeners, end up with. In fact, there are probably more tanks, in more homes, in this category than any other.

There is no reason that you can't play with the lots of different ideas as well as plant species. Spend some time on the internet looking at different tanks, see what appeals to you and draws your eye. People often show me their tanks apologetically, saying, "Well, it's not a competition tank." That doesn't matter. A tank doesn't have to be a winning "contest" tank to bring years of enjoyment. What matters is that you like it.

Other individuals, like the well-known aquascape artist Oliver Knott, enjoy being playful with their aquascapes. Oliver doesn't take himself or his aquascapes too seriously; he knows this should be fun for the aquarist as well as for the viewer. Most of us want to enjoy getting our hands wet and working with lots of different plants and designs. After all, we're gardeners. Enjoy it.

If and when you decide you want to try a formal aquascape of one style or another, the best way to learn this art is by producing many small aquascapes. Small aquariums under 10 gallons make the whole process more affordable, and if the tank doesn't work out the way you'd hoped, it's easy to dismantle and start again. The best aquascape artists in the world have done many, many 'scapes. It takes time and practice to perfect this art.

This Diorama-style aquascape gives the feeling of looking through large old trees toward forest and mountain in the background. Aquascape Luis Carlos Galarraga.

PALUDARIUM

Another type of garden under glass that has become quite popular is the paludarium, which is a tank set-up with part land and part water. The land part is typically filled with terrarium plants and small epiphytes while the water portion is planted as any planted aquarium would be. Often the maker will include a small waterfall powered by a pump.

Sometimes these tanks are strictly plant tanks, while other people populate them with fish or small amphibians. Dart frogs are a favorite, but require some specialized care. Several types of newt and fire-bellied toads do very well in such a set-up and are inexpensive and quite easy to maintain.

It can be a challenge to get the lighting right in these tanks, as too much light will burn the terrestrial plants, while too little will not allow the aquatic plants to grow. Some people choose to light appropriately for the terrestrial plants and use low light plants in the water section like *Anubias*, Java ferns, small *Cryptocoryne* species, and mosses. Now, with LED lighting available which can be placed directly over the water areas, it is possibly to light appropriately for both the terrestrial and aquatic areas, opening up the possibility of using many more species of plants.

A Fusion-style tank like the one shown here doesn't quite fit the category of Nature aquarium. It's certainly not a Dutch aquarium or a biotope, but it is a very pretty tank to enjoy in your home. Aquascape by Kaylan Bhowmick.

This paludarium was built
in a small desktop tank.
Aquascape by Cory Hopkins.

11

PUTTING
IT ALL
TOGETHER

NE OF THE BEST WAYS to learn more about aquascaping in terms of both technique and what appeals to you is to browse through the many aquascape photos online. Simply Googling the word *aquascape* will bring up thousands of images to stimulate your imagination.

If you want more in-depth information, visit the Aquatic Gardeners Association Contest Web site, where you will find not only every aquascape entered in the contest since it started in 2000, but also details on layout, materials, and equipment, provided by the aquarists.

There are also a number of aquatic plant forums on the internet where you can follow people's tanks from set-up though maturity, and many Facebook groups where people share their tanks as well. Get involved with these groups. You'll learn a lot.

Following are several step-by-step guides to assembling an aquascape.

DESIGNING AND PLANTING A SMALL TANK

1. Before starting an aquascape, make sure you have all your materials close at hand. It is helpful to have a piece of paper or cardboard that is the same size as the tank, on which to play around with your hardscape.

2. Work out the approximate placement of the hardscape on paper until you are satisfied with the result.

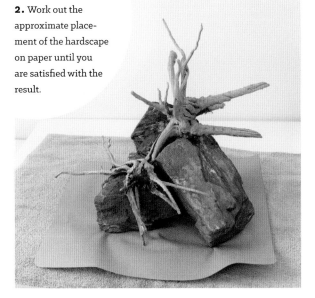

3. Dampen the substrate in the tank but not so much that you have standing water on the surface. This will make it easier to plant and also easier to fill the tank cleanly later on. Then transfer the hardscape from your practice area into the tank. You may find that you need to fill in more substrate in some areas, particularly behind rockwork.

4. Before you begin to install the first plant, prep all of them by cleaning them and removing them from their pots. Make sure you have your planting tools and a spray bottle of water at hand also.

5. Keep your plants wet by spraying them as you work. Cover them with plastic wrap if you need to step away or if it is taking you a long time. Aquatic plants must not be allowed to dry out.

6. Don't forget to spray the plants in the tank as you work too.

8. To keep the water from disturbing the plants or substrate, drip it from the tubing onto a rock, and then let it trickle down into the substrate.

7. Start filling the tank with water very slowly. Use tubing to siphon water out of a bucket. This tank could have used more plants.

FILLING A SMALL TANK

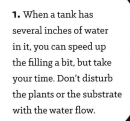

1. When a tank has several inches of water in it, you can speed up the filling a bit, but take your time. Don't disturb the plants or the substrate with the water flow.

2. When a tank is filled carefully via the bucket method, there is no reason for the water not to be this clean within hours of set-up.

3. Here the tank has had a chance to grow in a bit.

4. And here it is reaching maturity. *Ludwigia arcuata* (in the back) has been trimmed down so that it will grow bushier as it gets taller.

CREATING A PATH

1. Path-making is not very difficult. Use cardboard or stiff paper to divide the planting areas (dark) from the decorative sand (light). While you are filling in the substrate, hold the cardboard in place with small pieces of tape or stones. Fill evenly on both sides of the cardboard to keep it in place as the depth of the substrate increases. Place your path off-center and have it curve into the back, so that it disappears behind plants or hardscape for best effect.

2. When the substrate is as deep as you want it (planting areas should be at least 3 inches deep), remove the rocks if any were used and gently and carefully pull up the cardboard. You should have nice clean edges on your path.

3. In this project, I installed the driftwood hardscape after making the path. You could choose to install a hardscape before a path, especially if the hardscape consists of complicated rock work.

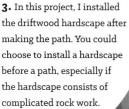

4. Here the tank is planted and filled. Because the two types of substrate have a tendency to mix, I chose to line the edges of the path with rocks wrapped in moss. They are very obvious in this first shot, but as the tank matures, they will start to look more natural.

5. The tank is maturing nicely and the moss has really filled in. The path has become small and the driftwood has practically disappeared. Hardscape that looks big and obvious when the tank is first set up can become overwhelmed quickly by fast-growing plants. Keep that in mind when planning your tank.

GETTING THE HARDSCAPE RIGHT

1. I take my time designing a hardscape. There is no rush and it is hard to change once the tank is planted and filled with water. I may change the arrangement several times before I get it the way I want it and start to plant.

2. Before filling a tank with water, I photograph it from all viewing angles and study my photos. I often see something in a photo that I didn't notice with my eyes.

3. The same hardscape from yet another angle. These three shots are part of the design process.

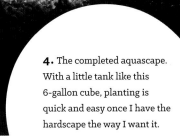

4. The completed aquascape. With a little tank like this 6-gallon cube, planting is quick and easy once I have the hardscape the way I want it.

PLANTING AND FILLING A LARGE TANK

1. Large tanks are more work, so really take your time. Here I have used petrified wood as the rock and thin manzanita branches. Thin branches like these don't hold up long-term, but they are inexpensive to replace and add a nice, light feeling in a scape.

2. With the substrate well dampened, plant all the foreground plants. Here I used a commercial soil-based substrate topped with a commercial calcined clay substrate. This helps reduce the amount of nutrients that are leached into the water column in the early stages, while still giving the plants a good, nutrient-rich substrate to grow in.

3. It takes longer to plant a big tank, so it is even more important to spray everything frequently to keep the plants from drying out.

4. With the foreground plants in place, start filling the tank. Use the same care that you used for the small tank so that you do not disturb the substrate. You can achieve this by trickling the water though a Python or other water change device slowly onto a shallow saucer, allowing it to gently overflow.

5. Close-up of filling the tank. I really mean fill slowly.

6. Once the foreground plants are fully submersed, you can plant your larger middle and background plants. You will need to continue spraying them until the water is deep enough to cover them.

7. It can be tedious filling a big tank, so use a chip clip to keep the hose in place while you do other things. Stay close by, though. You don't want to end up overfilling the tank and flooding your floor.

8. By the next day, the tank is settling in, though I still need to plant the small area where the bowl sat for filling.

9. The same tank over a year later.

10. The tank still older and pretty overgrown, though in a wild flower garden sort of way.

FILLING A NANO TANK CLEANLY

1. Tiny tanks like this 4-gallon nano tank can be filled cleanly too, but you need a different approach. Since there is no room to fit a dish, and it can be hard to trickle water slowly enough onto small rocks, place plastic wrap over the whole aquascape after planting and fill onto that.

2. I use a houseplant watering can to fill little tanks. This makes it easy to control the flow.

3. The plastic wrap floats up as the tank fills. Just keep pouring onto the wrap until the tank is almost completely full.

4. Remove the plastic wrap and the end result is another nice clean tank and undisturbed aquascape right from the beginning.

12

TROUBLE-
SHOOTING

EVEN WITH THE BEST CARE under the most experienced aquatic gardener, things can go wrong. Let's take a look at potential problems and how to prevent or remedy them.

ALGAE HAPPENS

Algae in an aquarium are like weeds in a terrestrial garden. No matter how hard we try, we can't totally avoid them. The goal for the planted tank should be to keep algae minimal, and if possible, nonvisible. The best way to do this is to make sure to balance light levels, CO_2, and nutrients in a heavily planted tank. The minute these factors get out of balance, a tank may end up with algae problems. Go back and re-read the chemistry chapter of this book. (See! I told you you'd need it!) It is easier to prevent algae problems than it is to solve them. However, if things do go wrong, there are methods you can use to get your tank back on track again.

You may read of various chemicals or antibiotics that you can use to resolve algae problems. For the most part, these products should be avoided. Many chemicals are toxic to some extent or other—always to algae of course, but sometimes to fish and even the humans who use them if they are not handled extremely carefully. And with antibiotics, there is always the chance of causing antibiotic-resistant strains of bacteria to develop, something the world doesn't need any more of. There is a safer alternative in almost every instance.

Planted aquariums are particularly vulnerable to certain types of algae during the first few weeks or months after the tank is set up. This can be a result of nutrients leaching out of the substrate, an imbalance between light, CO_2, and nutrient input, or with new aquarists, stocking too many fish in the tank or feeding them too much. Algae likely to be encountered during the initial life of the tank include green water, certain green filamentous algae, and diatoms. Later in the life of the tank, other types of algae can become problematic. These include black algae, blue-green "algae" and *Cladophora*.

Green water is a condition caused by an overgrowth of free-floating single-celled algae.

It is rarely possible (or useful) to identify algae at the species level, and sometimes even the genus can be guesswork. However, the common names of these groups of algae give us enough information to be able to deal with them effectively in the aquarium.

Green Water

Green water is caused by unicellular suspended algae that does not settle on surfaces, but instead turns the water cloudy. Often the cloudiness is bright green, though in the beginning stages it can just look a bit hazy. Green water is particularly common in tanks with soil-based substrates, but can show up in any tank, especially those that are stocked with too many fish too early. The reason is the same in either case—too much ammonia from either fish waste or released from the substrate, and not enough phosphate available to balance it. The problem is particularly common in tanks with very bright light, but once it gets started, it can be difficult to get rid of it.

Water changes seem not to help very much with green water problems. Often you can do a 90 percent water change, have the tank look pretty good right after the water change, and 24 hours later, it looks like pea soup again. The good news is that green water is not dangerous, to either your plants or your fish, and although unsightly, it is serving a purpose by slurping up excess ammonia. The bad news is that once green water is established, even balancing out your nutrient levels will often not get rid of it.

One effective, low-tech way to treat a green water infestation is to black out the tank for several days. Do a large (90 percent) water change to reduce the algae load in the water. Turn off any supplemental CO_2 and make sure there is plenty of surface agitation, either by adding an air stone or powerhead, or by raising the spray bar of the filter return. Turn off the lights and wrap the tank in heavy, opaque blankets or other material so that no light gets in. Leave the tank wrapped for three days. Don't peek. Don't feed your fish or worry about them. They will be fine for three days without food. In many cases, when you uncover the tank, the water will be sparkling clear again.

Micron cartridges for canister filters can also be used to mechanically filter out green water. However, these cartridges clog quickly, so you will need at least two of them, one to be in the filter while you soak and clean the other thoroughly, following manufacturer's instructions. The problem is that micron filters make the water look great while they are running, but if even one cell of algae is left behind, it propagates quickly and the tank is green again, soon after the micron cartridge is removed.

A sure bet for curing green water is an ultraviolet (UV) sterilizer. This is just a tube with a strong UV light inside it. The water moves through the tube, using the flow of either a canister or sump-style filter, or a dedicated power head or other water pump. The UV light kills unicellular algae as it passes by. Because there is no particulate matter to trap, the UV filter never becomes clogged nor does it need frequent maintenance the way a micron filter does. It can run on the aquarium indefinitely. The problem with UV filters is that they are another piece of equipment to buy for the purpose of solving what is often a one-time problem. I have one and haven't used it in over 15 years, but sometimes people get so frustrated with green water that it is well worth it for them to buy a UV filter.

Catfish in the genus *Ancistrus* can be effective at keeping small amounts of green dust algae under control. They are great algae eaters in the planted tank. However, some individuals can be a bit rough on some plants so only introduce them in tanks with tough plants.

Green Dust Algae

As its name implies, green dust algae will coat plants and glass with a dusting of green powderlike algae. The coating can become quite thick at times. This is a common problem in newish tanks and, fortunately, usually transient.

A common cause is a CO_2 level that is too low for the amount of light on the tank. Green dust algae can also be a sign that the nutrient levels are out of balance in the tank. The first thing to do is make sure that the tank has an adequate CO_2 level. Then check nutrient levels to make sure nothing is running low between doses.

When you've made any tweaks necessary to the system, wipe the algae off everything you can. Dust algae can be removed easily with any scrubby tool meant for algae removal. You can usually remove most of what has settled on the plants just by rubbing the leaves between your fingers.

Once you have "dusted" your tank, do a very large water change (90 percent) to remove as much of the algae that is now suspended in the water as possible. This is not the same type of algae as green water and won't stay suspended in the water; rather, anything left in the water will just settle out on surfaces and start to grow again. It may take several rounds of wiping the tank down then immediately doing a large water change before you get dust algae under control, but it rarely returns once the tank is mature. *Ancistrus* species can be very helpful in eating this type of algae.

Catfish in the genus *Otocinclus* have a sucker-type mouth and teeth designed for scraping. They use these teeth to remove algae from various surfaces including the glass.

Diatoms

Diatoms have the same dusty properties as green dust algae, but are not true algae, and have different causes and solutions. Like green dust algae, diatoms tend to be a transient problem in newly set-up tanks, coating everything, including plants, with a covering of brown dust. The organisms can be removed following the same methods as for green dust algae. Catfish in the genus *Otocinclus* and nerite snails are excellent helper animals to get the tank sparkling clean once the majority of diatoms are removed.

Filamentous Algae

There are many types of filamentous green algae. Many of the softer types can show up during the early months of a newly planted aquarium, especially any with a rich soil substrate, which may be leaching nutrients into the water column.

As is true when trying to reduce all types of algae, the first thing to do is to make sure that adequate levels of all nutrients are present in the aquarium. Pay special attention to providing plenty of CO_2. Make sure that there is also good water flow throughout the tank. Then manually remove as much algae as you can.

Some types of algae can be removed by hand, but for capturing smaller bits, an old toothbrush is a great tool. Catch the algae in the brush and twirl it around like spaghetti on a fork. You'll get most of it. Also, as for other types of algae, do a large water change and then make sure to dose your nutrients to keep the levels adequate for good plant growth.

Filamentous algae is best kept in check on an ongoing basis with grazing animals. Shrimp, especially Amano shrimp and cherry shrimp, are at the top of the list; however, some fish, like livebearers and certain barbs, can be helpful too.

Later, as your tank matures, other algae problems can crop up. While very small amounts of algae can be found in almost every planted aquarium, nuisance levels of algae are almost always the result of poor tank maintenance, a nutrient imbalance, or an imbalance between nutrient input, available CO_2, and light levels.

Black Brush, Staghorn, and Other "Black" Algae

Black brush and staghorn are actually in the family of red algae even though their color in the aquarium typically ranges from steely gray to black when they are alive. Most species are confined to marine environments. Unfortunately, the few that do make their homes in freshwater are especially problematic in the planted aquarium.

Black brush algae grows in short tufts from almost any surface in the tank including plants, hardscape, equipment, and even the silicone sealant at the corners of the tank. The glass tends to be the very last surface colonized, and I certainly hope you take care of it long before that happens. Staghorn algae is also a red algae, but it is branchy rather than growing in tufts of straight strands. It also tends to be a little lighter gray. Both types of algae respond to the same treatment methods, so we can discuss them together.

Horned nerite snails feed on algae in a tank. They are named for the multiple horns protruding from their shells. ◄

Several different animals can be used to keep soft filamentous algae in check. ◄

Black brush and staghorn algae are often seen in tanks with fluctuating CO_2 levels or not enough CO_2. This means they are common in low-tech tanks, especially if the aquarist is also running too much light over the tank. It really pays to make sure you have a good CO_2 delivery system on your tank and good water movement so that the CO_2 gets to all parts of the tank.

All black algae attach very strongly to whatever surface they are on. They can be very difficult to scrub off manually, and even the tiniest speck will regrow if you don't kill it. On plastic equipment, it is easiest to take the equipment out of the aquarium and soak it in 1 cup of bleach in a gallon of water. The bleach will effectively kill the algae, which you can then scrub off with an algae scrubber or other abrasive tool. Finally, soak any equipment that has been in contact with the bleach in a bucket with a good dose of dechlorinator before returning it to the tank.

The bleach treatment can also be used for rocks, but I would not suggest its use on porous materials like wood, as it would be hard to get all the bleach back out before returning it to the tank, and chlorine is highly toxic to your fish and invertebrates.

There is a relatively safe chemical that will kill black algae, is much less toxic, and it breaks down very quickly. That is hydrogen peroxide (H_2O_2). It is available in spray bottles at the pharmacy or grocery store and is a fantastic tool in the war against black algae. The

Amano shrimp should be a regular part of every planted tank for routine algae control.

Many barbs are good at eating filamentous algae. The advantage of long finned rosy barbs is that once they have taken care of the algae problem in your tank, they are easier to catch than those with normal length finnage.

best way to thoroughly clean wood that is really covered with brush algae is to remove it from the tank, thoroughly spray all surfaces with hydrogen peroxide, let the wood sit a while, then scrape off the algae with a dinner knife. Don't use too sharp a knife or you'll cut the soft, wet wood. You just want to scrape off the outer layer. Rinse away any debris and the wood is ready to be returned to the tank.

Hydrogen peroxide can even be used safely inside the tank without removing plants or animals. Draw the water level down as low as possible, then use the spray bottle to spot-spray the brush algae on anything not easily removed from the tank and now above the water level. This is the best way to get it off the silicone if it has started to grow there too. Let the spray sit for about five minutes, then refill the tank. No rinsing is needed. In a day or two the algae will turn red as it dies, and in a few more days it will start to deteriorate and fall off.

You can even spot-treat areas under water if you turn off all circulation in your tank for a few minutes. Use small amounts of hydrogen peroxide in a small syringe, and squirt it right onto the algae spots. Just don't use too much hydrogen peroxide in the water at any one time.

Black brush algae is impossible to remove from any but the toughest plant leaves, such as *Anubias*. Those can be treated just like hard materials in the tank and sprayed with hydrogen peroxide. For softer-leaved plants, you will just need to allow the plants to grow new leaves in their freshly adjusted environment and trim the infested leaves off.

Once you have cleaned up your tank as much as possible, banded garras and Siamese algae eaters are the best animals to keep black algae beaten back. Shrimp may help with tiny amounts, but they are ineffective for bad infestations.

Blue-Green Algae

Blue-green "algae" (cyanobacteria) is actually a photosynthesizing bacteria and can definitely become a pest in the planted aquarium. The freshwater type is usually blue-green in color, though occasionally you see strains that are a different color. It has a distinctive musty smell that can sometimes be noticeable even walking near the aquarium. It will roll off the glass or other surfaces in sheets, with very little pressure.

Cyanobacteria is rarely seen in newly set-up tanks and tends to be a sign that things have gotten rather badly out of kilter in a tank. Often it indicates that the aquarist hasn't been keeping up with proper tank maintenance. If cyanobacteria is in just one area of the tank, the cause may be poor circulation that allows a build-up of uneaten food and detritus in that area. If that is the only problem, improving the circulation by trimming plants, vacuuming the area with a siphon, or placing a powerhead in that area can solve the problem. Blue-green algae can also be a sign that nitrate is at a very low level in the tank in relationship to the other available nutrients.

No matter the cause, wipe the cyanobacteria off as many surfaces as possible. It can usually be easily wiped even off fairly fragile leaves. If it is on the substrate, it may be necessary to scoop just that very surface layer off to remove it. Once you've removed as much as you can, do a large water change, siphoning out as much of the cyanobacteria pieces as you can. Usually, cyanobacteria can be cleared up using the black-out method described for green water.

Obviously, once you've cleaned everything up, you should get your nutrient dosing back on track. As with all other types of algae, the better and faster your plants are growing, the less chance for weeds to take over, so keep those nutrients up, do your water changes, and supplement with CO_2 except in the lowest light tanks.

Their rasping mouth parts make it clear why banded garras are so effective at removing algae from a tank. ▶

Green Spot Algae

Green spot algae is typically seen down the road in planted aquariums. It is more common in tanks where the tap water is a little harder, though it can also show up in tanks with softer water. The harder the water, the harder you will find it to remove the spots. They are easiest to remove from the glass using a single edge razor blade. My favorite tool for this is a paint scraper with a fresh blade. These are fairly inexpensive, with blades that are easily replaced and with a nice solid handle.

Remember that whether you are using a safety razor or a paint scraper, these are very sharp tools. Handle with care and don't cut yourself. Unfortunately, it's just about impossible to remove these spots from plant leaves, even *Anubias*, so your only choice will be to remove affected leaves.

The most common causes of green spot algae are low phosphate, low CO_2, or a photoperiod that is too long. Get those things in order, and you should be able to manage around green spot algae.

Black brush algae colonizes leaf edges and thus cannot be scraped off without damaging the plants. ▶

Cladophora

Cladophora is another type of green, filamentous algae, but it is more commonly seen in mature tanks. It is easy to differentiate from other filamentous algae because it has a "crispy" feel. If you pull the strands apart, you will even hear a faint snapping sound. This type of algae is very frustrating as it seems to like the same aquarium conditions that aquatic plants like. In fact, *Cladophora* is often imported from another tank via plants, so inspect plants carefully before putting them in your tank.

The best thing to do with *Cladophora* is to manually remove every bit you can find. It doesn't fall apart easily, so most of it can be removed either by hand or with a toothbrush. Make sure your nutrient levels are in balance and that you are supplying plenty of CO_2. Make sure that your lights are not too strong and that the photoperiod is not too long. Once you have most of the algae removed from the tank, your algae-eating animal crew should be able to keep up with it.

CLOUDY WATER

During the initial stages of tank set-up, the water may become cloudy. This can happen because you filled the tank too quickly and disturbed the substrate, or because you did a major rework of the tank that included moving or planting many plants. Fortunately, this type of cloudiness will clear on its own in a few days. The more fine particles in the substrate you have used, the longer it can take, but there is nothing dangerous about it. Simply wait it out.

Another type of cloudiness is caused by a bacterial bloom in the water. This sometimes happens if the aquarist is too quick to add too many animals to the tank, and the biological filter can't keep up with the increasing load. In this case, you should check both your ammonia and nitrite levels daily. If they are elevated, do large water changes to keep them down to safe levels for your fish. You can also use an ammonia-locking water treatment product (such as Prime) to keep the water safe for your fish.

Another useful measure is to ask a friend or your local aquarium store if you can borrow a used sponge filter from one of their tanks to import more good bacteria into your system. Even squeezing the dirt out of active filter media and pouring it into your own filter can help jump-start the process.

It is rare to have a bacterial bloom in an older tank, but if you do, it means trouble. Something is rotting in the tank and needs to be found and removed quickly. It can be a larger fish that has died in a corner, unnoticed, and is decomposing, or it can be that someone has grossly overfed the fish. This is, unfortunately, a common occurrence when people go on vacation and ask someone inexperienced to feed their fish. It is the biggest reason that I suggest minimal or no feeding while you are on vacation. Hungry fish do fine and recover quickly when you come home. Overfeeding can lead to dead fish and a stinking mess upon your return.

A surface skimmer is useful for removing any surface film as well as pesky duckweed and plant trimmings.

DUCKWEED AND BLADDERWORT

Also under the category of garden pests are two aquatic plants: duckweed (*Lemna* species) and bladderwort (*Utricularia gibba*). Both spread quickly and can be a nuisance in a tank.

Duckweed floats on the surface of the water. Some people don't mind small amounts of it, but if the cover gets too heavy, it robs your aquarium of light and sucks nutrients from the water. It is particularly a problem in tanks that are not supplemented with CO_2; in such situations, duckweed has the advantage of absorbing CO_2 from the air, while it steals nutrients from your other plants.

Duckweed can be managed by skimming the surface with a small fish net, but you'll never get it all out that way. Small powerhead-driven surface skimmers, either commercially available or homemade, can remove every last bit from the surface for you.

Bladderwort is an even bigger problem, because it doesn't stay on the surface, where it is easily skimmed, but winds itself through stem plants in all parts of the tank. It is a common hitchhiker, both from other people's tanks and on stem plants that are grown commercially outdoors in many parts of the world.

The only solution to bladderwort is to try hard not to introduce it, or when it, inevitably, does find its way into your tank, be merciless in removing every tiny bit as soon as you see it. This is not a good place for using a toothbrush as bladderwort is very fragile, and every tiny piece broken off is perfectly capable of growing into a whole new plant. Instead, carefully remove every piece with your fingers, trying hard not to break it, every time you see it. Bladderwort is the bindweed of the aquatic world.

NUTRIENT DEFICIENCIES

People often want to know what specific deficiencies cause specific types of damage to their plants. While it is true that deficiencies can cause some recognizable damage, remember that there can be complex causes for leaf damage too. Too much of one mineral in the water can block the uptake of another. Too little of one may make the plant unable to access another even if it is present. Toxicity can also cause leaf damage that may mimic a nutrient deficiency. The accompanying illustration should therefore be viewed as general information.

The fact is that if you know what's in your tap water, dose other nutrients as suggested elsewhere in this book, provide adequate amounts of CO_2 and moderate amounts of light, and do regular water changes of 50 percent or more, you should not run into problems of nutrient deficiencies. If you do, rather than trying to figure out exactly what is missing, look at your system holistically and try to bring everything back into balance.

Signs of nutrient deficiency.

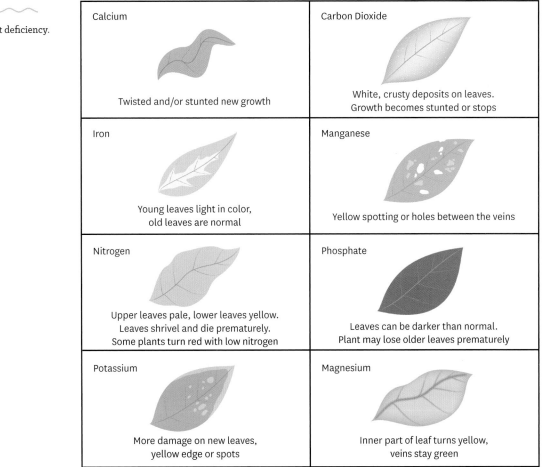

Calcium	Carbon Dioxide
Twisted and/or stunted new growth	White, crusty deposits on leaves. Growth becomes stunted or stops
Iron	Manganese
Young leaves light in color, old leaves are normal	Yellow spotting or holes between the veins
Nitrogen	Phosphate
Upper leaves pale, lower leaves yellow. Leaves shrivel and die prematurely. Some plants turn red with low nitrogen	Leaves can be darker than normal. Plant may lose older leaves prematurely
Potassium	Magnesium
More damage on new leaves, yellow edge or spots	Inner part of leaf turns yellow, veins stay green

RESOURCES

I hope that this book has given you the information that you need to get started in the fascinating world of aquatic gardening. It is a form of gardening that anyone can enjoy, year-round, in a minimal amount of space. Even the corner of a desk is enough. I also hope that you choose to continue to learn more about this wonderful world as you get your hands wet more often. To that end, here is a list of resources, both on and off the web, that I think are some of the best available to help you learn.

ASSOCIATIONS, CLUBS, AND SHOPS

The Aquatic Gardeners Association

www.aquatic-gardeners.org/

The AGA is an international organization, over 30 years old, dedicated to aquatic plants and aquatic gardening. It publishes the only full color English language magazine dedicated specifically to these subjects. The magazine is a benefit of membership. The AGA holds a large online aquascaping contest each year and a live convention every other year. The AGA also maintains a Facebook page where over 8000 people worldwide engage in discussions of aquascaping and keeping planted aquariums: https://www.facebook.com/groups/AquaticGardeners/.

Local aquatic plant clubs

Not every area has one, but if you are lucky enough to be in an area that does, by all means join. These groups attract the most serious aquatic gardeners and you'll learn a tremendous amount at their meetings. The URL for many local plant clubs can be found on the AGA Web site.

Local aquarium clubs

Most areas of the country have local general aquarium clubs. Don't pass these over, because most of them will have at least a few members who are also involved in aquatic gardening at some level. Most of these clubs have Web sites, monthly meetings with speakers, and regular auctions of plants and fish raised by members. This is a great way to buy plants from people who have personal experience growing them in tap water similar to yours.

Independent aquarium shops

Independent shops are more likely to have the best-quality tanks, equipment, and hardscape materials as well as the best selection of plants. If they don't have what you want, ask them; they can most likely order it for you. If you have a store that specializes in planted tanks near you, and there are a few scattered across the country, by all means support them with your business. These people are the ones who will be there to support you if you run into problems.

Web Sites

There are so many Web sites specializing in aquatic gardening that it can be overwhelming. By all means browse around any that appeal to you, but listed here are the sites where I am sure you can get good, reliable help if you run into problems.

The Barr Report

http://www.barrreport.com/

This is the only site that charges a fee to access some areas, though other areas on the site are free and open to all. The advantages of membership are worth the price. There is minimal advertising, and they keep on top of spam. The moderators are extremely knowledgeable and are very good about making sure that people are treated respectfully. There is a tremendous amount of good information available in their archives.

Flowgrow

http://www.flowgrow.de/db/aquaticplants/

Flowgrow is a German forum, but its aquarium plant database is the most accurate and up-to-date available. This database can be accessed in English as well as German. Should you want to participate in the forum there, that is also possible using a web browser, like Chrome, that will automatically translate for you.

Aquatic Plant Central

http://www.aquaticplantcentral.com/forumapc/

This is one of the earliest aquatic plant forums, and it is quieter than some. To me, that's a benefit, as some of the larger ones are so busy it's hard to keep up with them. There are knowledgeable folk here who will steer you in the right direction and a nice database of information on aquarium plants.

The Planted Tank

http://www.plantedtank.net/forums/

If you want a forum that is really hopping, this is one of the biggest. Again, there are knowledgeable folks and tons of material to look through.

UK Aquatic Plant Society

http://www.ukaps.org/forum/

This is one of those "local" groups I talked about, though it's only local if you consider the United Kingdom "local." The Society also has an excellent Web site and forum available to all, no matter where you live.

BOOKS

Amano, Takashi. 1994. *Nature Aquarium World*. Neptune City, New Jersey: TFH Publications.

This book was followed by two others (1996) and then a larger volume that combines works found in all three (2011). The late Takashi Amano, his Nature aquarium layouts, and his fantastic photography of these tanks are what have made aquatic gardening the rising star it is today. You do yourself a huge favor by buying at least one of these books, simply for the inspiration you will find in them. They are heavy on photos and light on information, but a real feast for the eyes.

Kasselmann, Christel. 2002. *Aquarium Plants*. Malabar, Florida: Krieger Publishing Company.

This is the English edition of a German book. Even though it was published more than a decade ago, it is the only book that is accurate for the identification of a wide range of aquarium plants. The author is one of the foremost authorities on aquarium plants worldwide. She has extensive experience with these plants both in the field and in the home aquarium. Some plants have had scientific name changes since this edition of the book was written, but it is still an essential part of every serious aquatic gardener's library. The book is no longer in print, but is still available for reasonable prices from a number of sources.

METRIC CONVERSIONS

GALLONS (U.S.)	LITERS
1	4
4	15
5	19
6	23
7	26
10	38
15	57
20	76
30	114
50	189
75	284
90	341

INCHES	CENTIMETERS
1/10	0.3
1/2	0.13
5/8	0.16
1	2.5
2	5
3	7.6
4	10
6	15
18	45

FEET	METERS
3	0.9
4	1.2
7	2.1

FAHRENHEIT	CELSIUS
78°F	26°C
82°F	28°C

VOLUME	
½ teaspoon	2 milliliters
1 cup	250 milliliters

ACKNOWLEDGMENTS

I would like to thank all of the wonderful people who have taught and encouraged me through the years of my journey with aquatic gardening. In particular, I'd like to thank Claus Christensen, past director of Tropica Aquarium Plants, who first contacted me years ago on CompuServe, before the internet as we know it today. From Denmark to the United States, we struck up a fast friendship, and he has been an invaluable resource to me over the years, introducing me to many wonderful people in the world of aquatic plants, across the world.

I'd also like to thank Christel Kasselmann, who is one of the most knowledgeable people I know when it comes to aquatic plants, not only in the wild, but also in the aquarium. I wouldn't have been able to learn a fraction of what I have without her help, friendship, and mentorship.

Thank you to the following people for being kind enough to read, review, comment, and advise on various portions of the book: Tom Barr, Phil Edwards, Scott Hieber, Vaughn Hopkins, Erik Olson, Cheryl Rogers, and Kris Weinhold. Their help was invaluable.

I'd also like to thank all the people of the Greater Washington Aquatic Plants Association, who were kind enough to let me descend on them to take (and model for them as well!) many of the "how-to" photos I needed for the book.

Thanks to all the people through the years who have allowed me into their homes to photograph their lovely aquariums, and thanks, also to all in the aquatic gardening community who rallied round to help me fill in missing photos, whether your photos were chosen in the end or not. You were all wonderful.

Last, but certainly not least, I want to thank my family, especially my husband, Dave, for putting up with all the time, travel, wet floors, and piles of rocks in the basement that have come to be part of my life with aquatic plants. Without them, this book would not have been possible.

PHOTO CREDITS

All photos by the author unless otherwise stated here.

INDEX

ABOUT THE AUTHOR

KAREN A. RANDALL IS AN EXPERT on planted display aquariums and the propagation of aquatic plants. Her articles and photography have been published internationally. For many years she wrote the monthly column "Sunken Gardens" in *Aquarium Fish Magazine* and is now technical editor of the Aquatic Gardeners Association magazine, *The Aquatic Gardener*. She has traveled extensively to study and photograph aquatic plants in the wild. In 2003 she won the Northeast Council of Aquarium Society's Betty Mueller Award, a lifetime award for her outreach work and other contributions to the aquarium hobby.